Furniture Restoration Workshop

Furniture Restoration Workshop

KEVIN JAN BONNER

GUILD OF MASTER CRAFTSMAN PUBLICATIONS LTD

First published 1999 by
Guild of Master Craftsman Publications Ltd,
166 High Street,
Lewes,
East Sussex, BN7 1XU

Reprinted 1999

ISBN 1 86108 048 4

British CIP data
A catalogue record for this book is available from
the British Library

Photographs by Kevin Jan Bonner
Black-and-white line drawings on page 88 by Rob Wheele
Colour drawing on page 58 by Simon Rodway

Designed by Ian Hunt Design
Cover design by Wheelhouse Design
Typeface: Stone Serif and Gill Sans
Colour origination by Viscan Graphics (Singapore)
Printed in Hong Kong by Hong Kong Graphics Ltd

Contents

Introduction

When I was first asked to write this book I intended it to be a very simple exercise; take a dozen pieces of everyday tatty furniture and document the restoration of each.

I have read other restorers' accounts of their work on a piece of furniture, but I always feel ill at ease with their descriptions of events. They seem to miss out the most interesting parts of the process: the problems encountered, how they solved them and why they made the decisions they did. It all sounds too easy, the descriptions don't ring true. You are led to believe that the experienced furniture restorer's life is bliss, built on the infallible techniques and insight of years of practice. This is not my experience of the craft.

And so the germ of an idea grew – a book of restorations that showed what it was really like, warts and all. A book that did not leave out the gory details, the boredom, the good luck and the bad luck, the frustration, the hard work. A book that included all of the problems and that described the thinking behind the decisions made in order to solve those problems.

Of course, many of the projects would have been a lot easier to read about if I had omitted all this information, but they would not have been a true reflection of what a restorer really gets up to. So in the name of science, for the integrity of the book, and most importantly for your education, they remain.

I realize that I do not necessarily come out of this looking like a first class, slick furniture restorer who knows exactly what he is doing every step of the way, never putting a finger wrong. But then that is definitely not the aim of this book. As my grandmother always said, albeit rather imperfectly, 'You should always be wary of the perfect. They are obviously trying to impress you, therefore they should not be trusted.'

I wanted to make this book as worthwhile and as valuable to the reader as possible and after much deliberation set a number of goals that I felt the book should aim for.

The first was that the projects should be subject to as many different finishes and techniques as possible to make the book as rich in information as it could be, and for the same reason I included a wide range of furniture types.

Since this book is for beginners to the craft, all of the items are inexpensive. I do not advocate restoring antique furniture until you have gained confidence and have tried out some of the necessary skills and techniques on 'junk' furniture.

I decided to use pieces of furniture that are commonly available, thinking that the reader should be able to find similar furniture quite easily by scouring their local junk shop, jumble sale or boot sale. So, if you are particularly impressed by one of the projects, you should be able to find a similar item of furniture and follow the procedures to a satisfactory conclusion. However, if you prefer, you can use the ideas, finishes and repair procedures, but apply them to a piece of furniture of your own choosing.

Once I had chosen projects, I decided that the book should also work as a course of study, so it starts with the simplest projects and ends with the more complex.

You will find, as you read through the book, that the information contained in earlier chapters is built upon, helping you to appreciate and understand the information in later chapters. By the end of the book you should have a good understanding of the most important of the professional furniture restorer's techniques and of the various tools and materials they use.

The book functions as a reference guide so that you can dip into various chapters to find out specific information, such as how to apply a wax finish or what criteria to use in choosing a new set of cabinet knobs. It also provides a catalogue of design ideas to inspire you to restore your own furniture.

And of course, if nothing else, it should be a good read. Even if the book does not inspire you to restore a single piece of furniture, I hope you will enjoy having an insight into the plight and the pleasures of the professional furniture restorer.

CHAPTER 1

The Process of Restoration

To give you a clearer understanding of the process of restoration, perhaps a closer look at the structures I have used for guidance would be informative. The structure of each chapter follows the process of thought that I work through in restoring furniture. There are four main steps, as follows.

1 Study the furniture. Looking at what we've got, I give a little background information on the project, explaining where the item came from and where it is intended to go. I also discuss the history of the type of furniture concerned.

2 Determine the brief, answering the question, 'What do you want to do with the furniture?' Do you just want to use it to learn how to french polish or are you interested in transforming it into a plant stand. Will it be used for food preparation or is it to impress your mother?

   Whatever your brief turns out to be, it will affect your later decisions about what type of finish to use and how much you wish to spend, so it is best to have it clear in your head.

3 Write out an action plan. This is where you map out exactly what you need to do in order to achieve the aims that you have set out in the brief.

4 Begin the restoration, working your way through the action plan.

Simple, isn't it? Except that the more work you do to furniture the more you uncover, and the more you see, the more you think about what's in front of you. And more often than not you have to change your plans in light of these discoveries.

This is not a failure as you will see on reading through the projects: it is the process that we go through when restoring. You can't tell what you are going to encounter when you start to restore a piece of furniture. What you find under the surface and how you feel about the furniture can change dramatically in a few seconds. All you can do is plan for the unexpected and be prepared to change course at a moment's notice.

Now, this is all starting to sound very complex which, in fact, it is. But the best way to understand what goes on is to follow the chapters, watch the furniture being restored, and absorb the thinking behind the actions, getting a feel for the principles behind the craft of restoration.

With each project you should pick up the more tangible craft skills, such as removing dents in wood, using coloured wax and applying spirit stain and, most importantly, the principles at work behind the thinking and the decisions made.

It is this information and knowledge that will enable you to become confident enough to make your own decisions about individual pieces and to restore them in the way that you would like to.

As you will see, each piece of furniture is different so each restoration will be different. This is what makes the craft so interesting. The processes and procedures that the restorer uses are altered and invented to fit the endlessly varying circumstances and problems that arise.

You have to make it up as you go along, but at the same time you must plan the process and think it through. Herein lies the paradox that makes the journey so much fun. You set out with your map (action plan) pointing in a certain direction but you can never be sure where you will end up or what you may encounter.

This book will lead you through some restoration journeys, showing you how they were mapped out and why certain decisions and preparations were made. It will also highlight the pitfalls encountered along the way and how they were skirted, or fallen into.

CHAPTER 2

Working Requirements

When first starting a course on furniture restoration, students of the craft will often ask the most perplexing questions. This, of course, is as it should be. Hopefully, during the course of this book, I shall be answering many of those questions. One of those most commonly asked by new students is 'What is the most important requirement of the furniture restorer?'

Work Space

The first requirement of the furniture restorer is a space to work in. Professional restorers use a purpose-built workshop to carry out their work. Amateurs tend to have a dedicated workshop – usually a shed or garage attached to their house – in which to carry out their hobby. I have used both, but I have to tell you that the best place to restore furniture is an open space such as a garden, patio or balcony. This is because the principal requirements of the furniture restorer's working environment are fresh air, good lighting and plenty of space to move around your furniture.

Of course, if you are trying to work during the winter months or a wet summer then there is no doubt that you will need a space to protect you from the weather and to store your equipment and half-finished projects. But don't use the lack of this sort of space as an excuse not to start work. It may be desirable, but it is not vital. All of the projects in this book were started and completed out of doors, over the summer months – and a very enjoyable time it was too.

Fig 2.1 *A collection of screwdrivers.*

Tools

Apart from a space to work in, you will need a small number of simple hand tools, such as screwdrivers and hammers. These are to be found in most homes.

Fig 2.2 *Assorted scraping tools.*

If you are desperate to spend some money then you could do with a collection of scraping tools, some wire wool, an assortment of sandpaper, and a selection of paint brushes.

Finding which scraping tools work the best for you is a matter of trial and error, so the wider the range you have available, the better. Use 120 grit sandpaper for all purposes: finer grades become clogged too quickly and coarser grades are too rough. For the same reasons, medium grade wire wool is the most suitable for all applications. For brushes, go for the mid-price range.

Fig 2.4 *Various grades and forms of sandpaper.*

Cloths

You will also require an unlimited supply of cloths, not only for some of the finishing techniques, such as waxing or french polishing, but also for any number of odd jobs such as cleaning off the last vestiges of stripper from surfaces, cleaning up spillages and wiping your hands.

Fig 2.3 *And more scraping tools.*

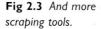

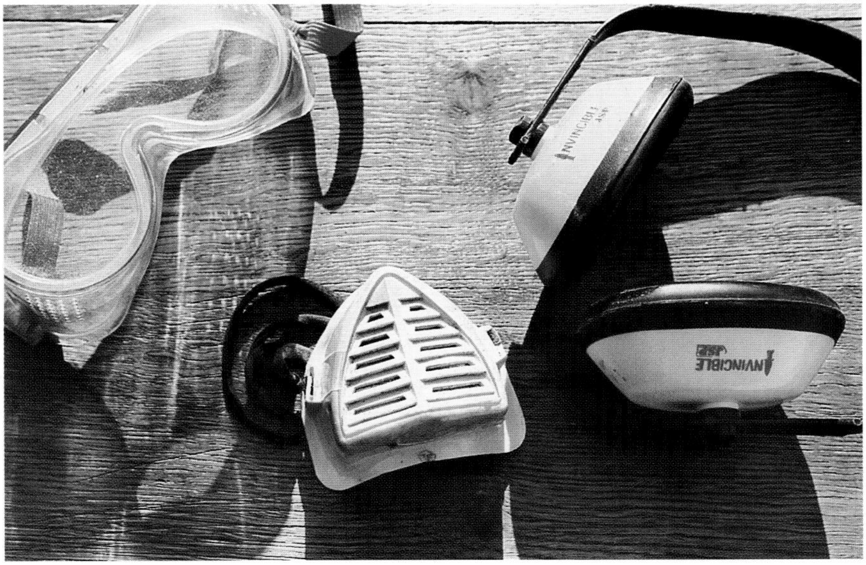

Fig 2.5 *Think safety – invest in protective clothing and equipment.*

Safety Equipment

Lastly, but most importantly, you will need some safety equipment. I know professionals who consider it an insult to wear eye protection or masks, and sometimes it can be a real pain having to wear them, but I can assure you that there is nothing as painful as a poke in the eye with a screwdriver smothered in paint stripper. Or a severe attack of dermatitis or the dozens of other complaints that can be avoided with a little forethought.

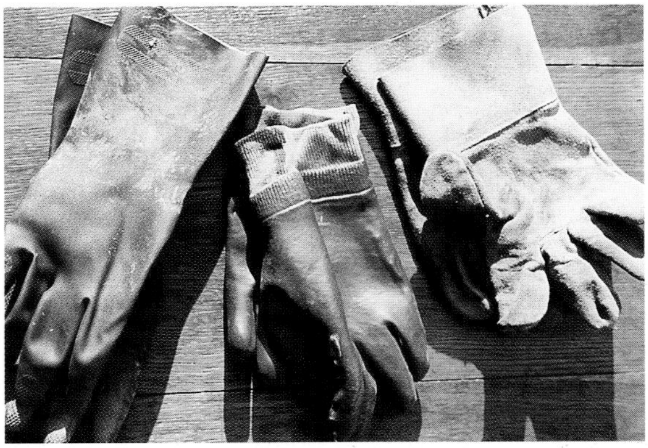

Fig 2.6 *And don't forget gloves!*

Invest in your health. Think safety before you start work and use the appropriate protective equipment and clothing.

In addition to safety equipment, it is wise to have a well-stocked first aid box, and to know exactly where it is kept. Try to keep it somewhere that is accessible. It is no help having to climb a ladder to reach the first aid box when you have twisted your ankle or knee, or having to hunt around in the dark looking for the eye bath that you last saw under the stairs the previous Christmas.

You will have accidents, hopefully not too frequently or too serious: the best way to make them as painless as possible is to prepare adequately for them.

Essential safety equipment

- A well-stocked first aid box
- Dust mask
- Eye protectors
- Selection of protective gloves

CHAPTER 3

Materials

The finishes and other materials required for restoration will depend on the particular finish that you are applying to your projects. These items are best bought as required. If they amount to anything that is out of the ordinary, such as pieces of veneer or new knobs for a cabinet, then their purchase should be included in your plan of action (see Chapter 1).

Even in a short period of time you accumulate a range of half-used finishes and other proprietary concoctions. It is wise to supply yourself with a strong box and a safe home for this stuff to keep out prying fingers. Be mindful that some finishes are inflammable, so don't store them under the barbecue or next to grandad's smoking chair.

Solvents

Every finish is constructed from two main elements: a solid and a liquid. The liquid is known as the solvent and is used to liquefy the solid. The solvent is also used to thin the finish and to wash brushes and clean up spillages. When the liquid finish is applied to a surface the solvent evaporates, leaving the solid part of the finish behind.

Understanding what the solvent of a product is will give you clues as to which products are compatible and which will not work together. However, even if two products do not contain the same solvent, for example oil stains and french polish, this does not mean that they should not be used on the same piece of wood, only that they cannot be mixed together when liquid. If you were to apply oil stain to wood and allow it to dry (that is, allow the white spirit to evaporate), there would be no problem in applying french polish over the top.

Components of common finishes

	Solid	**Solvent**
French polish	Shellac	Methylated spirit
Wax	Beeswax	Turpentine
Polyurethane varnish	Resin	White spirit
Water-based lacquer	Resin	Water

White spirit, turpentine and turpentine substitute

For our purposes there is no difference between white spirit, turpentine and turpentine substitute.

White spirit and turpentine substitute are man-made equivalents of the naturally occurring turpentine, which is obtained from certain pine trees.

Turpentine is very pungent and is toxic if inhaled or absorbed through the skin. It is also very expensive, but it is the solvent of choice for purists – and those of a masochistic tendency.

Turpentine substitute is much cheaper. Some purists, and many manufacturers, suggest you should only use pure turpentine when mixing wax polishes. This could be harking back to Olde Worlde Wisdom and respect for all things ancient, but there may be some value in eschewing white spirit because of its powdery residue. To my mind it doesn't really matter, but I do go along with the manufacturer's preferences.

Because these finishes, stains and varnishes have the same solvent they are compatible, and many times in this book I will mix these products to produce a new concoction.

Remember that white spirit is flammable, so any finishing product containing white spirit will be flammable.

Methylated spirit (denatured alcohol)

Methylated spirit is the solvent for all of the french polishes and for spirit stains. Having a common solvent makes these products compatible.

Methylated spirit also bears the distinction of being able to dissolve an applied, hardened french polish finish, so it can be used to strip these. (See Chapter 4, page 21 and Chapter 10, page 79.) It is also very flammable.

Water

Water is used as the solvent in emulsion paints, in some wood fillers, in water-based lacquers and in water-based paints. It is not only the cheapest of the solvents but also the most user-friendly.

Cellulose

Cellulose is the most volatile and the most flammable of the solvents – and it is very smelly. It is used in cellulose lacquers, in some wood fillers, and also in some specialist paints. It is worth noting that it is also the solvent for nail polishes and for many car paints.

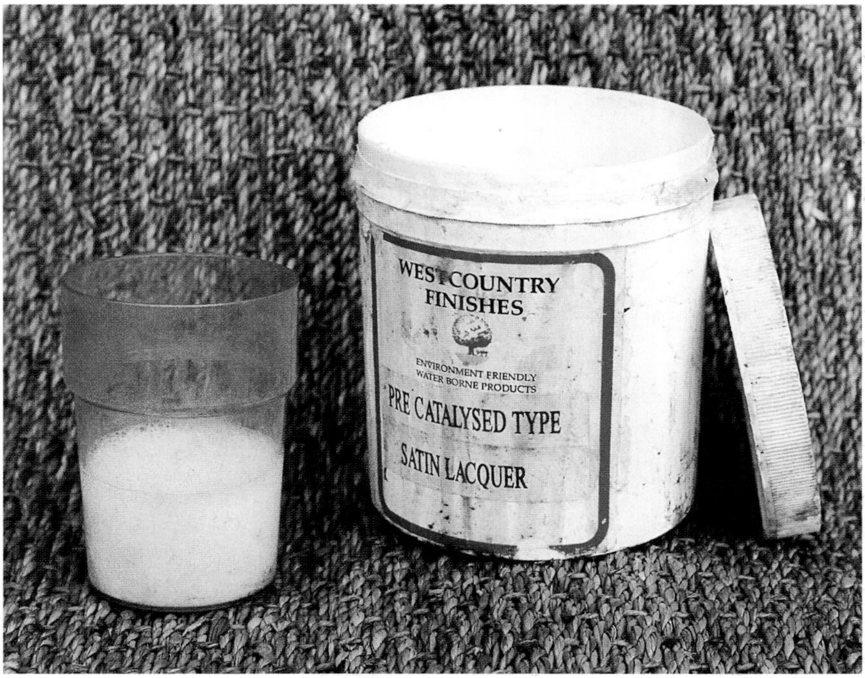

Fig 3.1 *A water-based lacquer: water is the most user-friendly solvent.*

Finishes

French polish

French polish is the traditional finish for much antique furniture and for 90% of the furniture found in junk shops.

French polish is made by processing the mortal remains of aphid-like beetles that infest certain trees in parts of Asia. The processing provides a thick, toffee-like resin, sometimes referred to as shellac. When cold and dry this resin becomes very hard and brittle. It is made liquid by the addition of methylated spirit.

There are dozens of different types of french polish available from trade suppliers, but in DIY shops you are only likely to find three different types: white polish, button polish and garnet polish, as listed below:

- White polish is a creamy, light yellow colour and dries clear. It is formulated to be used on light-coloured woods such as natural oak or pine.
- Button polish is a light brown/orange colour. It is formulated to be used on light brown timbers such as beech elm and light mahogany.
- Garnet polish is dark brown and is formulated to be used on dark woods such as walnut and dark mahogany.

However, just because the different polish types are formulated for use on particular woods, this does not exclude their use on other varieties.

All french polishes can be applied using a brush (see Chapter 9, page 76) or a rubber (see Chapter 10, page 82).

Spirit stains can be added to any french polish to create a coloured polish. Notably, black spirit stain is added to create an ebonizing french polish (see page 12), and a red/brown spirit stain is added to create a mahogany polish.

This very important quality is shown to best effect on the Chest of Drawers in Chapter 8.

Fig 3.2 *A selection of french polishes, with a french polishing rubber.*

This shows how spirit stains can be used to colour and obscure filler that has been applied underneath french polish.

French polish is easily scratched, and easily marred by water and heat. It should therefore only be used in select areas where it is protected from these damaging elements.

Polyurethane varnish

Amongst DIY decorators and woodworkers, this is perhaps the most popular and commonly available finish. It can be formulated for indoor or outdoor use, when it is sometimes called yacht varnish. There is a bewildering number of shades and three levels of shine: gloss, satin and matt. It usually has a thick, treacly consistency but there are non-drip varieties which take on the composition of jelly. All of these varieties can be found on the shelves of DIY stores.

Polyurethane varnishes are slow-drying but hard-wearing, being resistant to water, scratching and heat. This makes them ideal for areas subject to hard wear, moisture and heat.

The common factor in all polyurethane varnishes is the solvent, white spirit. Clear varnishes can be coloured by the addition of an oil stain as described for the Bedside Cabinet in Chapter 6.

Polyurethane varnish does go 'off' and become slower drying if stored for long periods of time. Avoid this by always using fresh varnish. The varnish is best applied in lots of thin coats, using a decorators' brush. Always rub down between coats with 600 grit wet and dry abrasive paper.

Waxes

In its simplest form, wax polish consists of a block of unadulterated beeswax (straight from the hive) softened to a butter-like consistency by steeping in turpentine overnight.

To this basic wax polish can be added various ingredients to produce specific finishes, as listed below:

- extra turpentine will produce a brushing or liquid wax (see page 53)
- water and a little soap will give a wax 'cream'
- white paint will produce a liming wax (see page 130)
- oil stain will give a coloured wax (see page 67)
- soot and dust from the vacuum cleaner added to a coloured wax will give an antique wax.

All of these preparations can be bought off-the-shelf at DIY stores if you prefer.

Oils

There are a number of different oils available to woodworkers. They all have a similar composition and consistency, and can all be thinned with white spirit and coloured with oil stains. The application method for each oil is the same: rub or brush the oil into the wood, allow it to soak in and then wipe off the excess with a clean cloth.

Edible vegetable oil

This is the simplest of the woodworking oils. Being undoctored, it has the simplest chemical make-up, and it is also readily available, easy to care for and safe to use with foods.

I have used vegetable oil to finish the Fruit Bowl in Chapter 4.

Linseed oil

Linseed oil has been used as a wood finish for centuries and is still used in countless woodfinishing preparations and recipes. There are two types: boiled and raw. Raw linseed oil is used as a lubricant in the french polishing process (see page 87); it is thinner and easier to use than the quicker-drying doctored oils. However, time restrictions sometimes demand use of the quicker drying oils. Raw linseed oil can be doctored in a number of ways, depending on the manufacturer. One method is to boil the oil, reducing its viscosity and removing some of the lighter ingredients. Another way is to add chemicals to increase the speed of drying. Usually, both methods are used to produce boiled linseed oil. Both types can be used as finishes in their own right or as part of a finishing process.

I have used linseed oil to finish the Chest of Drawers in Chapter 8.

Vegetable oil blends

Danish oil, Scandinavian oil, antique oil and finishing oil are all vegetable oil blends that have been subject to other processes and to which additives have been introduced, to make them quicker-drying, easier to use or more resistant to wear.

I have used Danish oil to finish the Country Chair in Chapter 5.

'Oil from another country'

This is an oil that I am very fond of using. It is my own concoction and I use it in exactly the same way as the other oils described. If you would like to experiment with it, mix equal quantities of polyurethane varnish, linseed oil and white spirit and stir well before use. I often use it as a cheaper alternative to shop-bought Danish oil.

Water-based lacquers

These are relative newcomers to the woodfinisher's shelf. They answer the demand for an environment- and user-friendly woodfinish. As the solvent for water-based finishes is tap water, they provide a non-smelly, non-flammable, healthier alternative to the more traditional finishes. They should be applied with a brush.

I have used a water-based lacquer to finish the Telephone Chair in Chapter 12.

Stains

There are four types of stain available to woodworkers:

- oil stains
- spirit stains
- water-based stains
- chemical stains.

Oil stains

For the DIY woodworker, these are the easiest stains to obtain. Typically, shops will sell a range of about a dozen ready-mixed cans of stain in various wood colours. These can be added to all white-spirit-based products. Oil stains can be expensive if used in quantity, but they are the first choice for the DIY decorator and woodworker.

Essentially, oil stains consist of pigment, oil and white spirit. They should be shaken thoroughly before use as the pigment sinks to the bottom of the can.

Spirit stains

These are invaluable if you are using french polishes as they can be added to the polishes to achieve a required colour. They can also be added to some cellulose finishes. They are not as easy to come by as oil stains, but are available from specialist suppliers in ready-mixed or powdered form.

There are dozens of colours to choose from and these can be easily mixed to produce different shades. However, they will fade in bright light, and many are toxic.

Water-based stains

There is a good range of bright colours available in water-based stains. They are non-toxic, environmentally friendly and usually child safe. Be aware that water-based stains will raise the grain of wood. I haven't used any in these projects but some craftspeople will use no others. Generally speaking, I prefer not to use water-based stains unless I am using a water-based finish on top. The reason for this is that water can have detrimental effects on most traditional finishing systems.

Chemical stains

These are archaic preparations and are used by many woodworkers to give an authentic finish when following antique methods or restoring antique furniture. They are available from specialist suppliers.

Many chemical stains are highly toxic, so personally, I don't like having them around. If you are intrigued by them, I suggest you experiment with one or two once you have become proficient with oil and spirit stains.

Strippers

Chemical stripper

I have already mentioned that methylated spirit can be used to strip french polished finishes (see Chapter 10). The most common method, however, is to use a caustic chemical stripper, varieties of which are readily available in DIY shops. They do vary in price, and some are thicker than others, but whatever their advertising may say, they are much the same product in different cans. I always advise to buy the cheapest.

The chemicals used in these strippers are very strong and will burn your skin so be careful: use gloves and read the instructions in Chapter 5 on page 28.

Fig 3.3 *Various paint and varnish strippers.*

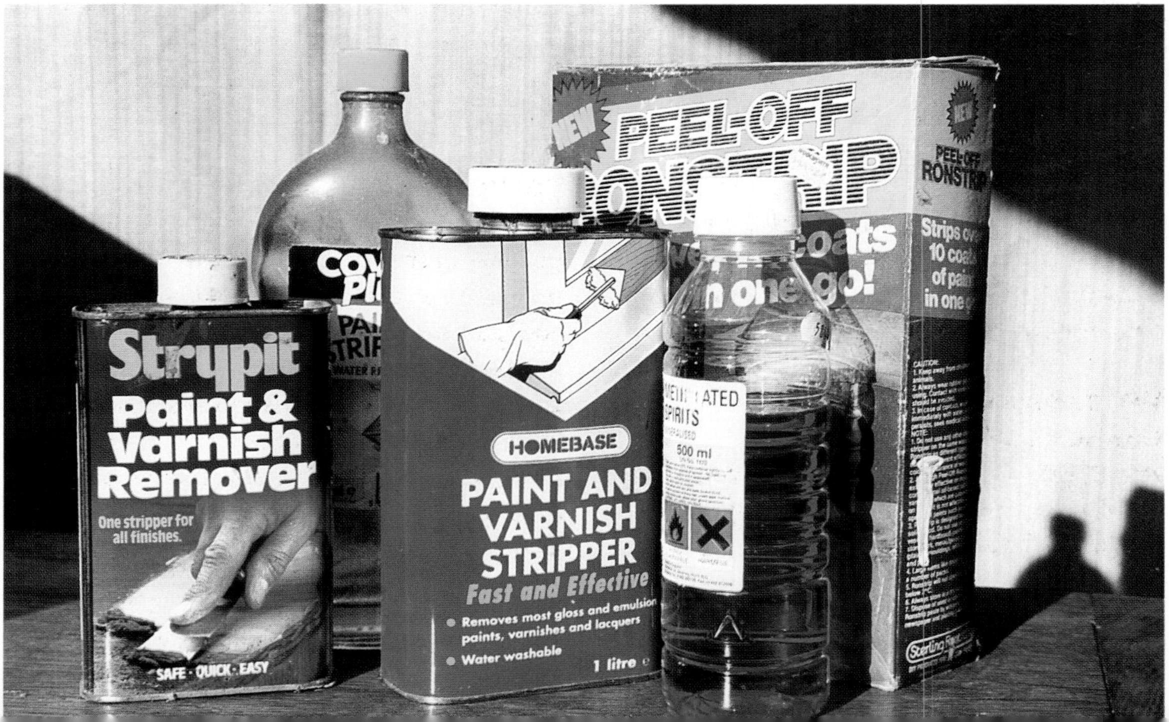

Stopping and Fillers

'Stopping' and 'filler' are fairly interchangeable terms though 'stopping' is generally used to refer to smooth fillers used for hiding small blemishes such as recessed nail heads. The term 'fillers' usually refers to stronger formulations used for bigger jobs.

The important thing to remember about all fillers is that, in order to achieve a smooth, even finish, you must overfill the area you are filling and rub the filler smooth with abrasive paper after it has dried.

Fillers can be formulated for indoor and outdoor use. Rather than buying a different colour for each type of wood, my advice is to buy a small tin of natural filler for use on all woods. Once the filler has been applied to the wood, rub it down with abrasive paper, then colour it with spirit stain or oil stain, applied with an artists' brush.

Wood stopping is not very strong, so it should only be used in protected places or for small areas. (See Chapter 4, pages 24 and 25, and Chapter 9, page 74.)

Plastic wood

Plastic wood usually has a cellulose solvent, which makes it quick-drying, and contains sawdust to give it a coarser composition. It is a very popular filler in the building and decorating trades where it is used for structural woodwork. However, I don't consider it suitable for use on furniture as it does not provide a fine enough finish.

Car body filler

This is a favoured filler of mine. It has two components: the filler and the hardener. Once these have been mixed together, the filler must be used before it goes hard, which is usually within 20 minutes. It is a cheap, very hard finish and dries very quickly. The only drawback is that it has a light grey colour when dry and sanded and applying stain to this base colour can sometimes cause problems, particularly on lighter woods. On such occasions I use two-part wood filler.

Fig 3.4 *Car body filler.*

Fig 3.5 *All glues have their own particular advantages and disadvantages.*

Two-part wood filler

Wood filler is more expensive, and slightly coarser than car body filler, but it is more favourably coloured, being a light brown. Again, it is a two-part filler, and has a hardener which must be mixed with the filler in the same way as a car body filler.

I have used wood filler on the Drop-Leaf Table in Chapter 7.

Glues

All glues are different and they all have their own particular advantages and disadvantages.

Polyvinyl acetate adhesive (PVA)

This is my personal favourite and fills 97% of my woodworking needs. It is very user-friendly, cheap and readily available, ready-mixed in both outdoor and indoor varieties. PVA is a water-based glue and is both heat- and water-soluble.

PVA works best when the wood to be joined is very close-fitting, without any gaps in the joints. As you may imagine, when restoring old furniture you occasionally come across joints that are not very close-fitting. On these occasions I use urea-formaldehyde.

Urea formaldehyde (Cascamite)

If the wood to be joined is not close fitting, I use this type of glue as it will fill large gaps and not lose any of its adhesive qualities.

Cascamite is sold as a white powder which must be mixed to a thin paste with water. Unfortunately, once mixed, it must be used within 20 minutes. I always keep a pot of it on the shelf for special occasions, but not for general use.

Animal glue

Older readers will remember animal glue (sometimes known as Scotch glue) as the smelly stuff that looks like thin toffee. It has to be heated up in a special 'pan' and wiped onto the surfaces to be joined. It sets as it cools. In certain situations it can make sticking two pieces of wood together the easiest job in the world; at other times you need a PhD in Applied Choreography in order to get the glue onto the wood and the wood assembled before the glue goes cold.

I only use this glue when absolutely necessary, for example, when authentic 'old technology' is required for restoring the best quality antique work. In the meantime, stick with PVA and Cascamite.

Animal glue is heat- and water-soluble.

Brushes

Artists' and decorators' brushes

Small, artists' brushes are invaluable to the furniture restorer, particularly for applying

Fig 3.6 *Artists' brushes are useful for work on small areas.*

Fig 3.7 *You can never have enough brushes.*

stain to filled areas when you are trying to achieve an invisible mend (see page 50). For applying finishes and stains, use larger decorators' brushes. Old decorators' brushes can be given a second life, by using them to apply chemical stripper.

Wire brushes

There are two types of wire brush that I use: a suede brush and an engineers' wire brush.

A suede brush is a small, brass wire brush made for cleaning suede shoes and clothing. Suede brushes are soft enough not to damage wood but firm enough to clean out old, softened finish from the wood grain and around intricate or complicated mouldings and turnings. (See Fig 7.3, page 49.)

An engineers' wire brush, on the other hand, is used to remove rust and to clean metal. To compare one with a suede brush is to compare a wolf with a poodle. They can be used to scrub the grain of woods, particularly oak, prior to grain filling or waxing, for a particularly textured effect.

Case Histories

CHAPTER 4

Fruit Bowl

FINISH: VEGETABLE OIL

I've chosen this project for the first chapter as it is an ideal starting point for anyone who is new to furniture restoration. Instant and easy results are to be had with just a minimum of effort, but there is still a lot to be learnt and important points to be considered in choosing an appropriate finish.

CONCERNING *Bowls Generally*

Wooden bowls and similar wooden kitchenware items are popular subjects for restoration; they form a family of woodware that demands a particular type of finish. Such items include chopping tables, breadboards, rolling pins, wooden knife handles, cheeseboards, storage jars, salad bowls and fruit bowls. These items are different from household furniture because they come into regular contact with food and therefore require frequent cleaning to maintain hygiene. However, they rarely get mentioned in books on furniture restoration – an omission that I believe to be an oversight.

CONCERNING *This Bowl*

This bowl has been floating around my parents' home for what seems like forever. Nobody can remember where it came from or when it first made an appearance.

I remember the bowl having a number of uses in my youth, amongst them holding nuts, fruit, salads and snacks. Latterly it has been donated to my own household where it has been used to hold felt-tip pens, Plasticine and various other knick-knacks. So it has a rich and unconventional history, which has resulted in the bowl looking as it does today – worn out and mucky!

It is a very plain and simple design: turned on a lathe from cherry wood and finished with a thin, french polish-type finish. Judging from the colour, which is no longer in its original state, it is probably button polish.

Although french polish can be a very beautiful finish, it is not very hard-wearing, nor is it water-resistant. Therefore, over the years the polish on this bowl has worn away. Consequently, when it is washed, the bare wood becomes soaked and takes a long time to dry out. If this treatment continues, the colour of the wood in these places will fade and the bowl may even split.

It has already been discoloured in a number of places – probably from the aforementioned felt-tip pens. Also, some candle wax has been spilt on it. These are typical blemishes found on many other types of furniture.

TOOLS AND MATERIALS
For This Bowl
(*approx.*)

- Methylated spirit, 250ml (9 fl oz)
- Oil stain, 5ml (⅕ fl oz)
- Wood filler, 10ml (⅖ fl oz)
- Sunflower oil, 250ml (9 fl oz)
- Medium grade sandpaper
- Wire wool
- Chisel: 6mm (¼in)
- Old rag
- Cotton cloth
- Artists' brush: No 2

Safety

Methylated spirit is flammable, so take the usual precautions and don't smoke or work near an open flame.

The Brief

The brief is simple. At the moment the bowl is tawdry and unappetizing to the prospective fruit eater. We need to render it waterproof, hygienic and wholesome.

We also need to put back some of the colour as it is looking anaemic and lacklustre.

The Plan of Action

1 Strip off old finish.
2 Remove blemishes.
3 Apply food-safe finish.

The Restoration

Stripping

The stripping technique that I'm going to use for this project is very simple. It is employed only when dealing with thin, french polish-type finishes and relies on the fact that french polish is easily dissolved by meths.

Pour some meths into a small bowl, tear off an egg-sized wad of wire wool, dip it into the bowl of meths and rub it gently into the

Fig 4.1 *Using wire wool and methylated spirit for stripping the bowl.*

Safety

Tiny metal splinters from wire wool can become lodged in the skin. These can be exceedingly irritating and difficult to remove. Avoid this by wearing gloves.

finish. After about 10 seconds, the polish will soften and be removed by the scouring action of the wire wool. When the wire wool becomes clogged and ineffective, turn it over and use a clean section. Finally, wipe the surface clean with a fresh piece of wire wool followed by a clean cotton cloth.

Scouring with wire wool has a wonderful effect on the wood, giving it a good general clean. Apart from removing the old polish, it also dispatches some of the lesser felt-tip marks as well as the grubby stains that have collected over the years.

With a little experience this process can work remarkably quickly. But remember, it only works on a thin, french polish finish. Other types of finish require a chemical stripper (see page 28).

The stripping took 12 minutes.

Removing the blemishes

Black marks are a common form of blemish on furniture. We shall meet many more during the course of this book. There are three main types of black mark; ink stains, burns and, less obviously, from a chemical reaction that

Tips

Don't place metal containers on old wooden furniture, particularly if they are liable to get wet. This will cause black marks to be left.

Fig 4.2 *Removing black marks by scraping.*

Fig 4.3 *Removing drips of glue with a chisel.*

sometimes takes place between natural acids in the wood and any metal objects such as pots or plant stands that are placed on it.

Whatever the cause of black marks, my initial attempt at removing them is always the same: I try to remove the blemish by gently scraping it away with a sharp implement. I use a 6mm (¼in) chisel, but a sharp knife can be just as effective.

Tips

Not to be denied the explanation of wax removal, I'm going to tell you anyway. The efficient removal of candle wax relies on the fact that it, and other waxes, are softened by white spirit. Just wipe over the offending area with a cloth dampened in white spirit and the wax will disappear like ice cream in the sun.

This scraping process relies on the assumption that the stain does not go very deeply into the wood. (For information on removing more stubborn stains, see page 81.) All that is needed is for the very top layers of the wood to be scraped away. Always scrape in the direction of the grain and finish the job with fine grade sandpaper.

In the case of my fruit bowl the black marks did not penetrate deep into the wood and were therefore removed very easily.

The entire scraping process took approximately seven minutes.

Removing the wax drips

The spot of wax turned out to be a mis-identification: in fact, it was a spot of glue. This is a pity as I was intending to explain to you how to remove wax drips (a common problem) from furniture.

If *your* candle wax turns out to be glue, then it needs to be carefully scraped or lifted away with a sharp chisel or knife.

Adding to the plan of action

Now that the wood is stripped and all traces of blemish have been removed, we can carry on with the refinishing. Unfortunately, I encountered an unforeseen problem. While I was stripping, that rather unattractive and highly visible knot started to annoy me. I had tried to turn a blind eye to it, in the hope that I would grow to appreciate it, but it kept nagging away at me. It was an unpleasant focal point that I could no longer ignore. Further investigation, general prodding and poking, revealed an unwholesome soft centre to the knot and before long, the knot became a hole in need of filling – and another job was added to my original plan of action.

There is a wide variety of wood fillers on the market (see page 14). For this bowl I used a proprietary, water-based, smooth, interior grade, very light brown stopping. Its principal ingredient is clay, to which it is similar in texture and application. I wiped a finger full of filler into the hole.

I waited for the filler to dry (around 45 minutes outside on a warm day), sanded it lightly, then coloured the area with oil stain applied with an artists' brush. This turned the Frankenstein of knots into a 'Woodworkers Monthly' pin-up.

Golden Rule

When filling in a hole, always overfill; this is a basic principle of furniture restoration because all fillers will shrink slightly as they dry. Whatever the type of filler, a smooth, level surface can be achieved by rubbing down with a fine grade abrasive paper after the filler has dried, though large repairs may require a number of applications to get a perfect result.

Applying the new finish

So now we are left with a naked fruit bowl, free of old finish, black marks, felt-tip pen splodges and glue blobs masquerading as wax drips, with a knot that woodworkers dream of finding in their bowls. All the hard work has been done, the tedious stripping and the clever fixing, all culminating in the most satisfying (and often the easiest) part of the project – the finishing. We are looking for a finish that:

- will be easy to care for;
- is suitable for use with foods (i.e. will not poison anyone or impair the taste of the food;
- is capable of standing up to frequent washing; and
- will protect and, hopefully, enhance the look of the wood.

The finish I have chosen to solve this equation is ordinary edible vegetable oil (as used for cooking). This is a standard finish and procedure for any wooden item that is used in the kitchen. Use a clean cotton cloth to rub this into the wood, and after about 30 minutes, wipe off any excess. This bowl looks perfect with just one application, but if the wood is very absorbent you may need to apply three or four coats.

Vegetable oil finishes bear the distinction of being the oldest woodfinish known to mankind, with a history stretching back to cave dwelling times. Although the use of this finish has stood the test of time, it is not very resilient on a day-to-day basis. Each time the bowl is washed, it will need a 'top up' oiling to maintain the finish.

Problems

A few weeks later and the bowl was still looking wonderful – until it needed a wash . . .

Fruit bowls normally only need a cursory wipe over with a damp rag. However, I had not reckoned with God's revenge for a misspent youth – children. My teenage son has never given more than a cursory wipe to anything in his life, so a slightly soiled fruit bowl seemed an ideal job for him. Of course, the usual ineffectual wipe was immediately replaced by gut-busting all-out war with a scouring pad in an attempt to remove 'that stain in the middle of the fruit bowl', my lovingly disguised knot.

That, of course, was my mistake. If I had thought about it, I would have realized that the form of interior filler and the method of colouring I used would not survive frequent or abrasive cleaning (though it would have been fine on a piece of furniture). A small oversight on my part. But then, as they say, hindsight is 20/20 vision.

Never mind. I scraped out the old, now soft and damp filler, and refilled the hole with a waterproof, exterior stopping. This has a slightly different composition to the original interior filler, being based on white spirit, and must be left overnight to dry. Once the filler had dried, I gave the bowl another wipe over with vegetable oil to finish.

The finished bowl in use.

CHAPTER 5

Country Chair

FINISH: DANISH OIL

We are often regaled with stories of how a piece of antique furniture worth thousands of pounds has been found in an old barn or attic. Consequently, the first thing I did when I moved into my present home was to spend half an hour in the loft, searching for the lost treasure that could bring boundless wealth and the end of all material want for my family and friends.

However, all I got, beside a bad case of attic-searcher's stoop, was this little gem. A rather tatty and abused country chair. I was so disappointed with my find that I left it right where I found it – until now. I have decided to turn this country chair into a chair to be used in the garden.

Allow me to explain. I have, for a long time, wanted some garden furniture. However, I am reticent; I dislike the white plastic stuff, my back senses that the average deck chair was designed for the Spanish Inquisition, and I don't like the financial or environmental implications of teak or iroko garden furniture. Accordingly, each summer I take an upholstered dining chair from inside to use as a seat in the garden – and very nice it is too. It is light enough to be carried around the garden to find the best spot to catch the sun, and it is comfortable. The trouble is that English summers are pitted with English rain. Invariably the chairs get left out overnight, soaked and ruined. And it's not only the rain: the upholstery is also in danger of becoming bleached by the sun and getting covered with suntan oil. This is where the country chair comes in.

It occurred to me that I should design and make a chair for the garden, in order to get

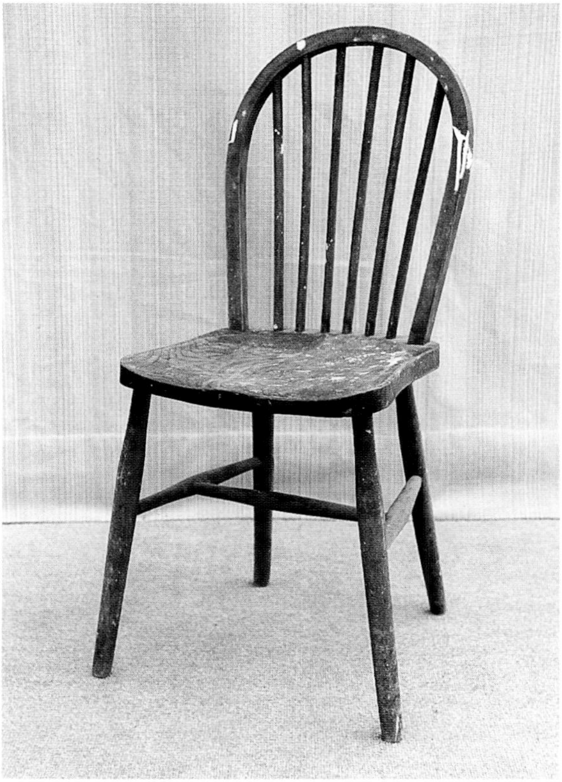

Fig 5.1 *The country chair, fresh from the attic.*

one that I could afford and liked. Whilst sketching a few designs, I realized that the solidly built, all wooden 'country' chair reposing in my attic would be ideal for the garden; all it needed was a waterproof finish. So, back into the attic I went to retrieve my chair for conversion into a country garden, sunbathing chair.

CONCERNING *'Country' Furniture*

There is a whole family of furniture that comes under the banner 'country'. Why it should be called country is open to debate. Undoubtedly it is an old term that is buried in history, folklore and the quaint marketing of the twentieth-century antiques dealer.

'Country' covers any piece of furniture that is more crude and rustic than the more fashion conscious and perhaps more refined furniture found in the town house. It often displays a vernacular quality that is rooted in simplicity and functionalism. Whatever the reason, the term has a certain logic and poetry to it and so it has stuck.

Country chairs come in many styles, the most famous being the Windsor chair. In days gone by, the craftspeople of different regions produced their own indigenous designs from locally sourced timber.

CONCERNING *This Chair*

This particular chair is a very simple and common design; indeed, it is still being made to this day. The seat is made from elm and the rest of the chair from beech. The hooped back was formed by heating the beech in a steam bath until pliable, and then bending it to the required shape. The other parts of the chair – legs, stretchers and spindles – were turned on a lathe.

The finish is a dark brown, french polish type. The chair could date from any time between 1880 and 1920. Even this range is a guess, based on the condition and colour of the chair (otherwise known as the patina).

The Brief

My desire is for a chair that I can use in the garden, that will withstand the rigours of hot sunshine, wet weather and oily suntan lotion. Plus, of course, the odd spilt vodka and orange (with ice please).

The Plan of Action

1 Strip with chemical stripper.
2 Stain with oil-based stain.
3 Finish with Danish oil.

TOOLS AND MATERIALS *For This Chair*

(approx.)

- Chemical stripper, 300ml (10½ fl oz)
- Methylated spirit, 250ml (9 fl oz)
- Oil stain 50ml, (1¾ fl oz)
- Danish oil, 500ml (18 fl oz)
- Chisel: 12mm (½in)
- Small knife
- Flat scraper
- Wire wool
- Clean cloths
- Paint brush
- Wire brush

The Restoration

Stripping techniques

I used methylated spirit to soften the old french polish finish on the Fruit Bowl in the previous chapter, and removed the softened finish with wire wool. Other types of finish and thicker french polishes require a more powerful stripper. For 90% of the furniture that I strip, I use a standard chemical stripper. These strippers are available from all DIY stores and the stores' own brands are usually the cheapest. They may be called paint stripper, varnish remover or even hard finish remover, but essentially they are all the same.

Brush the thick gel-like liquid onto the furniture. This softens the finish, allowing its easy removal with a scraper. Finally, scrub the wood with wire wool dipped in white spirit or meths, to remove any remaining finish, and to neutralize the chemicals in the stripper.

These are the bare instructions that you will find on the back of any stripper container. The old saying, 'a little knowledge is a dangerous thing', should be added to this for what they don't tell you is how painful, mind numbingly boring, back breaking and ultimately soul-destroying the task can be. Unless, of course, you pick up a few hard-earned tips from an experienced restorer . . .

The complete chair took me three hours to strip. However, it should be stated that I spread the stripping operation over a whole day. My technique is to listen to the radio whilst stripping, stopping at the end of each completed section for a cup of tea. Since the weather was exceptionally fine on this occasion, I also enjoyed a spot of sunbathing. If you find yourself getting bored, allow your mind to wander . . .

Stripping is a necessary and onerous task and has to be done well. You have to make it enjoyable, otherwise you will start to cut corners in your rush to get the job over and done with. Such measures will always show in the end product.

Before we start, it is best to expose a common mistake made by beginners. They tend to smother every part of the furniture in

Tips

These tips apply to all the projects in this book that require stripping.

Take care where you work. Strippers give off strong and noxious fumes so you need lots of fresh air whilst stripping. You also need lots of room so that you can walk around your project without bumping into things. Finally, you need good lighting. The place I favour above all others is the garden; the air is fresh, the space open and, in my case voluminous, and the lighting is unsurpassed. Failing a garden, an uncluttered shed or garage with the doors open, or a sparse room with all of the windows open will do.

Raise the project off the ground. Unless you enjoy crawling around on your hands and knees, place your project on trestles or an old table. Stripping is hard enough – there is no need to make it more difficult.

Supply yourself with a bench or side table on which to keep all of your equipment and supplies, and keep all of your materials in the one place. Otherwise, you will waste countless, frustrating hours searching for tools that have fallen in the long grass or that you have put 'somewhere safe'.

a thick and gluey layer of stripper, wait for 30 seconds and then start scraping the toxic gunge. Invariably, all parts of their (and their pets') anatomy becomes covered in this dripping mess, causing them to curse the day they were born. Learn from the mistakes of others – don't do it!

Golden Rule

Always strip just one small section at a time. Only use a thick layer of stripper on thick finishes. For thin finishes, a thin layer is adequate and far easier to work with.

Stripping the seat

Now that we are physically and mentally prepared, I shall describe the stripping operation that I used. Always decant the stripper into a ceramic bowl or dish and apply it with an old paint brush. I always apply the stripper to one small section of the furniture at a time. In this case I began with half of the seat, applying only a thin coating because it was a very thin finish. A thick application (which is often suggested in the directions on the stripper container) would make the job messy, waste the stripper and make it more liable to drip all over your skin.

The stripper dissolved the finish on the seat very quickly, allowing me to scrape it off with

Fig 5.2 *Applying a thin coating of stripper.*

Fig 5.3 *Slowly scraping off the old finish.*

a small, flat scraper, and transfer it to a piece of old newspaper for easy disposal.

Once the bulk of the finish, stripper and chemical gunge had been removed, I scrubbed the area with medium grade wire wool soaked in meths. This removed any remaining residue. It is important to use protective gloves during this process, otherwise you could literally work your fingers to the bone.

Because elm is a coarse-grained wood and the seat had some finish lodged in the grain, I continued my stripping by scrubbing the wood with a small wire brush (such as those used to clean suede shoes). This was effective for a short period of time, until the stripper stopped taking effect.

When this happens, the stripper needs to be re-applied. Give the area another very thin coating then wait until the stripper soaks in and becomes a little bit dry. How long you need to wait depends on the temperature. If you start scrubbing too soon, the wire brush will become clogged with the liquid gunge which will then just get rubbed around into other areas of the wood. The whole thing will become too messy.

Because the stripper is so thin, it will dry out quite quickly but the finish that is lodged in the grain of the wood will take on a sticky, dough-like consistency. If you start scrubbing with the wire brush at this stage, the gunge starts to clean off quite easily and cleanly.

If the wood shows a particularly coarse area of grain, as it did in this case, you may need to apply another thin coat of stripper and scrub again to remove the ingrained finish.

Tips

The wire brush will need cleaning from time to time, as it becomes clogged with gunge. This is best done by scrubbing the brush against the edge of a wall, and is most effective when the gunge is dry, so each time you need to use it, clean it thoroughly first. Beware of the dust and debris that flies off, as this can easily flick into your eyes or be inhaled; protect your eyes and cover your mouth.

Fig 5.4 *Stripping ingrained finish with a wire brush.*

Because my scouring action thoroughly cleaned the wood, I found it unnecessary to finish off with wire wool and meths.

I repeated the stripping on the other half of the chair seat. Between the spindles that make up the back of the chair, I resorted to scraping with a 12mm (½in) chisel and a small knife, before finishing off with the wire brush.

Stripping the spindles

The next part was the spindles. Beech is a particularly close-grained wood with a very smooth texture, so the spindles required a different approach from the elm seat. I coated two of the spindles and a section of the hooped back with stripper, then donned my gloves and rubbed the area with wire wool

Fig 5.5 *Stripping between the spindles.*

Fig 5.6 *Using wire wool to strip the spindles.*

dipped in meths. Mucky, but effective, and surprisingly quick. The back took about half an hour to strip.

Stripping the legs

The legs were the easiest; I followed the same process as I did on the spindles, using thin stripper, then wire wool and meths. This cleaned them up very quickly.

Staining

It would have been quite reasonable at this stage to give the chair a couple of coats of finish and be done with it, but the colour of the wood looked a little 'washed out' to me. This is frequently the case with old furniture. The wood didn't need a total change of colour, just a rejuvenation of its natural colour.

Fig 5.7 *Applying an oil stain to even up the colour of the chair.*

I decided to stain the chair with an oil stain similar to the colour of the chair. This does not change the colour greatly, but it does even out any light patches and the resulting colour looks very natural. In fact, it should not look like it has been stained at all. (See Chapter 3 for further information on staining.)

Shake the can vigorously to make sure the contents are well mixed, then pour a little stain onto a clean cloth and rub it gently into the wood. I worked methodically around the piece of furniture making sure each section was finished before moving on. I followed the same order as the stripping – seat, spindles, then legs. Turn the item upside down and view it from a number of angles to ensure that you have not missed any areas.

Fig 5.8 *End grain will soak up more stain than the rest of the wood, resulting in dark patches.*

Staining does not take long – the whole process took just 10 minutes – but do beware of soaking the end grain with stain as this will make it a lot darker than the rest of the furniture. The end grain is a lot more absorbent than the rest of the wood and will therefore soak up a lot more of the stain, resulting in dark patches. This is a tell-tale sign that the wood has been stained by an amateur or by one who does not care for the finer points of furniture restoration. Avoid this slur on your character by leaving the end grain until the staining cloth is almost dry, then rub it hard with the cloth to impart the colour.

Beware of staining your fingers; wear protective gloves.

Finishing

I used a Danish oil to finish my country chair. This is the simplest finish known to the woodworker, requiring little or no skill, but resulting in a very beautiful and practical finish. Beware! This finish is so simple and beautiful it can be addictive.

Danish oil is readily available in DIY stores, appearing under a number of different names including finishing oil, Scandinavian oil and antique oil. Danish oils are derived from natural vegetable oils related to those used for the Fruit Bowl in Chapter 4 and their appearance and application are very similar. However, the additives in these oils make them much more resilient, harder wearing and, most importantly for my project, waterproof. If you want, you can mix your own home-made Danish oil concoction, which I call 'oil from another country' (see Chapter 3, page 12).

Pour some of the oil into a jar and use a clean brush to apply it. Allow the oil to soak in for 10 minutes, then wipe off any excess with a clean cloth. Leave to dry for four hours before applying a second coat, if required. I often apply only one coat, but this depends on the wood. In this case I applied two. I also turned the chair upside down and gave the

Tips

If you are using this finish on furniture that is intended for indoors, you can finish off with a coat of wax finish. (See Chapters 7, 8 and 14, pages 46, 67 and 130, for more information on wax finishes.) However, a wax finish is not suitable on furniture intended for outdoor use as wax deteriorates in rain and heat.

Safety

Something as easy and pleasant to use as Danish oil has to have some drawbacks! A perverse quirk of Danish oil, and some other oils used in woodworking, is that any cloths used to apply it have a danger of spontaneously combusting if they are not allowed to dry in the open air. In short, do not screw them up and stuff them at the bottom of a rubbish bin or store them in a work box. Open them out and lay them on a bench or outside to dry.

Fig 5.9 *Finishing the chair with Danish oil.*

joints and the underside of the seat a good soaking as protection for whatever the weather can throw at it. Each application of Danish oil took only five minutes.

Once the oil has dried, wipe over any shiny spots with wire wool to dull them down.

So there we have it; a waterproof, sun-proof country chair. All we need now is an English summer to test it. When the oil gets worn out or washed away with the rain, just apply another coat of Danish oil to keep it protected and looking good.

Another bonus of the oiled finish is that any spillages of suntan oil get rubbed straight into the wood – nothing wasted.

The completed chair and inset, in contrast, the country chair fresh from the attic.

CHAPTER 6

Bedside Cabinet

FINISH: POLYURETHANE VARNISH

As I said in the introduction to this book, the first stage of furniture restoration is to spend some time collecting information and posing questions about your chosen project. From this information you should then form an action plan.

However, often it is not until you have spent some time stripping the project that you become fully aware of what is in front of you. That is what happened with this project. It is a common experience and illustrates a very important principle which is as well to become aware of as soon as possible.

Golden Rule

However much you try to predict what work is needed in the restoration of a piece, always expect the unexpected, keep an open mind, and don't be a slave to your action plan.

Fig 6.1 *The bedside cabinet as it came to me.*

CONCERNING *Bedside Cabinets*

One-third of our lives is spent in bed. This must make the bed and associated furniture the most used that we possess. Some beds require side tables whilst others require shelves and such like built into the headboard. Whatever your preference the fact remains, we all sleep a little easier knowing that our treasured piece of night-time paraphernalia is close at hand. Whether it be a glass of water, an alarm clock or a bedside lamp, you've got to have somewhere to leave your bits when you're in the land of nod.

CONCERNING
This Bedside Cabinet

This is a wonderful example of the way in which much furniture echoes architecture in its design. Plinths, friezes, columns, mouldings and pediments are all features that appear in classical architecture and have been echoed in furniture designs for centuries.

This small cabinet was donated to me by a neighbour, along with the Chest of Drawers in Chapter 8. Both were unwanted and due to be thrown out. It is rare that you find such high-quality mahogany and craftsmanship begging for a home, but people throw things out for all sorts of reasons.

The cabinet is well made from a richly coloured, solid mahogany, probably around 1900. It is finished with a standard french polish. The door hinges are a little loose but there are no signs of structural damage. The joints are firm.

The top has a large, circular black ring and the cabinet is very greasy and grubby, but both of these problems should be solved when the piece is stripped.

There is a blemish in the wood that is a common feature of furniture from this age; a white speckled effect in the grain. This is due to the process employed at that time, of rubbing plaster into the rough grain of a wood to create a marble-smooth surface for french polishing. (See Chapter 11, page 96 for more information on this process.)

Once the plaster was located in the grain, one of two further processes was employed to make it invisible. The wood was either stained, in which case the white plaster grain filler was coloured along with the wood, or wiped over with linseed oil, which made the plaster invisible and imparted a rich, dark tone to the mahogany.

Golden Rule

You don't really know a piece of furniture until it has been stripped. Be prepared for unexpected faults and blemishes.

The reason that the plaster has now become visible is that over the last 100 years or so, either the stain has faded or the linseed oil has dried out. So, the remedy to this problem is to apply a new stain or to wipe over with linseed oil. Both remedies require the finish to be removed.

The Brief

I decided to keep this as a bedside cabinet. My brother is a habitual bed junkie and needs a bedside cabinet to keep all of his nocturnal requisites. Plus, his birthday is looming. What better present can a furniture restorer give his bed-addicted brother? A dark mahogany bedside cabinet would sit perfectly in his darkened chamber.

Because he smokes (yes, in bed!) and keeps all of his loose change, cups of tea, boiled sweets and keys on his present bedside table, the finish needs to be robust enough to cope with these excesses. The colour of the mahogany is perfect so it does not need a stain. I think a clear polyurethane satin finish would be most apt.

The Plan of Action

1. Strip with chemical stripper.
2. Make plaster filler invisible by rubbing in linseed oil.
3. Tighten up screws on door.
4. Varnish with satin polyurethane varnish.

TOOLS AND MATERIALS

For This Cabinet

(approx.)

- Chemical stripper, 200ml (7 fl oz)
- White spirit, 300ml (10½ fl oz)
- White paint, 250ml (9 fl oz)
- Yellow paint, 5ml (¼ fl oz)
- Oil stain, 50ml (1¾ fl oz)
- Polyurethane varnish, 250ml (9 fl oz)
- PVA glue, 15ml (½ fl oz)
- Fine grade sandpaper
- Wallpaper stripper: 76mm (3in) wide
- Chisel: 6mm (¼in)
- Wire brush
- Brushes: 50mm (2in)
- Screws
- Domestic iron

The Restoration

Stripping

The stripping process for this piece was much the same as for the country chair, although the flat surfaces of the cabinet are a lot easier to strip. On these areas I used a 76mm (3in) wide wallpaper stripper. I began with the sides first then moved to the front, the top, and lastly the insides of the cabinet, resorting to the wire brush only on the mouldings and in the tighter corners where a wire brush can clean up most efficiently. I also used the wire brush to clean the brass door pull before I removed it. One of the bonuses of stripping furniture is that the stripping operation also cleans the furniture. All of those mucky corners that nobody has shone a torch in for many a year get the equivalent of an exfoliating scrub. In keeping with this cleansing operation, I always inspect the underneath and backs of furniture and make sure that all the dirt, dust and spiders, dead and living, are removed. If these areas look

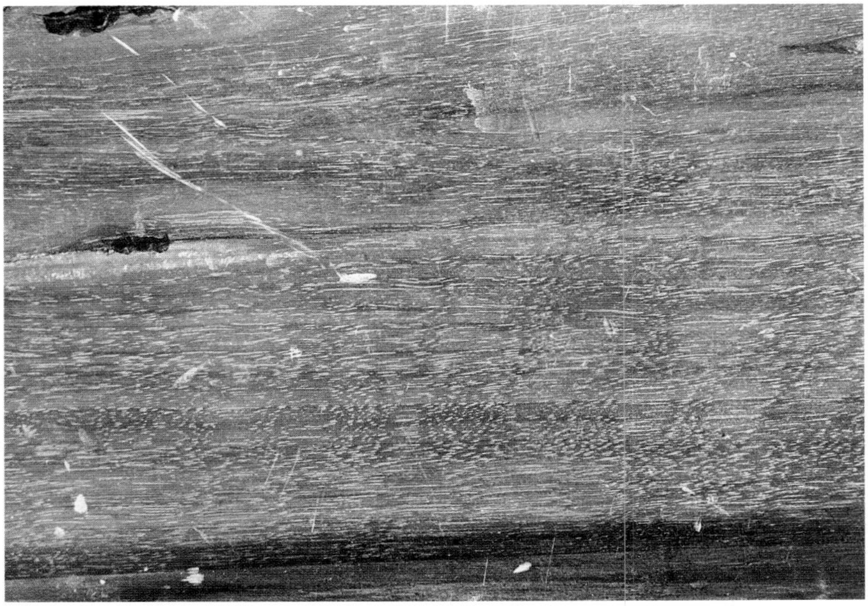

Fig 6.2 *The speckled effect caused by rubbing in plaster to fill the grain.*

Fig 6.3 *The long-neglected underside of the cabinet.*

particularly unpleasant – as they did in this case – I give them a thin coat of Danish oil to satisfy myself that all has been attended.

After this operation, I felt confident in bringing the cabinet into the house without fear of transporting woodworm or some unfamiliar or unclassified species into our living quarters.

Discovering Unexpected Faults

A close inspection also has other benefits; it forces you to examine the furniture very closely, with every nook, cranny and splinter coming under the microscope. Often, it is not until you have stripped a piece that you realize just what faults and blemishes exist . . .

It started with the plinth (the base of a piece of furniture). Whilst stripping, I realized that the plinth was not solid like the rest of the furniture, but pine with a mahogany veneer. This is a most annoying oversight on the part of the designer. Because the plinth rests on the floor, it is the part of the furniture that is most likely to be subject to dampness and to abuse such as being kicked or being dragged across the floor. On this cabinet, one side of the plinth had veneer that was peeling away and in need of repair.

Then, when I was stripping the old finish from the side of the cabinet, all of the colour was removed with the finish, revealing that some of the beautiful mahogany colour was

Fig 6.4 *The cabinet plinth, with its badly damaged and peeling veneer.*

Fig 6.5 *Stripping revealed the variation in natural colour.*

not as nature intended, but as the Victorian french polisher who finished the cabinet had intended (see Fig 6.5).

The wood here was a lighter and most inferior colour, so the french polisher had engaged in a little deception (or should that read 'craftsmanship'?) to match the inferior timber with the rest of the cabinet. This means that I will have to copy the Victorian's deception skill, and match the inferior, lighter areas with the prime mahogany.

The black ring on the cabinet top, which I had hoped would be removed with the finish, was still very much apparent with all the finish gone; in short, the stripping process had revealed much more than my original investigations had shown.

Changing the Approach

Perhaps most importantly, my closeness to the furniture over the day made me look a lot closer, and as they say, the more you look the more you see. The classical facade began to annoy me although it was what initially gave presence to the piece. It is almost like a model of a classical building. The more I looked at it the more it disturbed me, yet I couldn't put my finger on what was wrong.

Finally I realized what was niggling me. It was the overwhelming monumental, architectural look applied to the most humble and inconsequential piece of furniture. It was almost a pastiche, an outrageously pompous design for the most humble piece of furniture. Consequently, I cannot help viewing it with a little humour – and just a little distaste.

While staring at the cabinet over a cup of Earl Grey in the late evening and mulling over these thoughts, it dawned on me that I would like to respond to the cabinet's inherent deception and particularly to that air of architectural pomposity posing in a wimpy bedside cabinet.

I formed the idea that, although the outside should be returned to a standard mahogany finish to reflect the original intentions of the cabinetmaker, I would paint the inside of the cupboard with something outlandish like a bright pink or a yellow.

Alright, maybe it's not everyone's cup of tea, but it put a spring in my step at the end of a hard day's work. Besides, it will make the cabinet a little quirky, which is always pleasing to me and should also tickle my brother.

And so, I have to review and refine my original simple plan of action in light of the disclosures of the stripping process.

Plan of Action After Stripping

1 Remove the black ring from the top of the cabinet.
2 Tighten the hinges.
3 Repair the veneer around the plinth.
4 Stain 'deviant' wood and plaster.
5 Apply a polyurethane varnish to finish the outside.
6 Paint the interior some outlandish colour (yet to be decided).

In short, the original plan has changed out of all recognition.

Removing the black ring

We have already dealt with black marks on the Fruit Bowl in Chapter 4 and the remedy is the same here. The feint marks are very easily removed by scraping the black tentatively with the tip of a 6mm (¼in) chisel (see Fig 6.7).

Tightening the hinges

The hinges on the cabinet were very loose, and closer inspection revealed why; somebody had removed some of the screws. I removed another and took it to the local DIY store to get more of the same size.

I filled the holes with a little PVA glue, replaced the missing screws, and tightened the existing ones.

Repairing the veneer

There were no pieces of veneer missing from the plinth, so it was just a matter of gluing the old veneer back into place. Before gluing, I

Fig 6.6 *Stripping did not remove the black ring on the cabinet top.*

Fig 6.7 *Removing the black ring by scraping carefully with the tip of a chisel.*

ensured that the surfaces to be joined were clean and free of grit or any other obstruction that would interfere with the smoothness of the veneer. I did this by slipping a folded piece of fine grade sandpaper between the wood and the veneer and pulling the sandpaper back and forth, being careful to blow out all the dust that was formed in the process.

Following this preparation, I coated each surface with a thin and even coating of PVA glue (see Chapter 3). Allowing this to dry for about 10 minutes, I then used an ordinary domestic iron, set on a medium heat, to iron the veneer into place. Always place a sheet of paper between the iron and the veneer. This will prevent the iron sticking to the wood if there is any glue on its surface. It also allows the iron to glide over the surface easily, and keeps the wood from being burnt.

PVA glue is 'melted' by heat, so the iron melts the glue, forces the veneer flat, and pushes the pine plinth and the mahogany veneer together. The moisture in the glue saves the wood from drying out and shrinking or becoming too brittle. The bond is instantaneous, so no clamping is required.

Fig 6.8 *PVA glue is applied to both the pine ground and the mahogany veneer.*

Staining and obscuring 'deviant' wood

I chose to use a shop bought, red/brown oil stain (Indian rosewood from the Colron range) that experience tells me works well on mahogany. My first step was to give the entire piece an even stain, applying the oil with a sweeping motion, as described in Chapter 5 (see page 32). This stains both the wood and the plaster grain filler.

I then applied a coat of satin polyurethane varnish to the cabinet. To prepare the finish I stirred the tin well, decanted the varnish into a container and added 20% white spirit. I applied the varnish with a 50mm (2in) brush, brushing quickly so as not to disturb the stain on the surface of the wood.

Do not spend hours lovingly stroking and restroking varnish over a stained surface in an attempt to get an even coating. This will just remove all of the stain, mix it into the varnish, and make the whole surface blotchy and patchy. Remove any drips or runs after two minutes, with a dry brush.

Fig 6.9 *Using a clean cloth to apply an even stain to the whole cabinet.*

Fig 6.10 *Apply the satin varnish by brushing quickly over the stained surface.*

Once the varnish was touch dry (this takes about 60 minutes on a warm day), I gently wiped over the inferior, light-coloured areas with a cotton cloth dipped in some oil stain. Because I wiped over the varnish before it had completely hardened, the stain coloured the varnish, as desired, evening out the colour differences. I used a swiping motion to apply the stain, and allowed it to dry overnight.

Applying the varnish

My next step was to decant a little varnish into a container and thin it with oil stain. This creates a mahogany-coloured varnish. I applied this coloured varnish only over the light areas, using a different brush and a clear, uncoloured varnish to work over the dark areas. I repeated the process, allowing each coat to dry, until the light-coloured timber matched the good quality timber.

Golden Rule

There are no guarantees. Things do and often will go wrong. Learn from your mistakes.

On reaching the desired effect, I gave the whole project one final coat of clear satin varnish to seal it all in.

That was the theory anyway. In reality, I had to remove the whole patchy mess first time around and start again. This is because I made the mistake of being too impatient and applying the stain too soon. The varnish hadn't dried enough and the stain went on very blotchily. I learnt from this and the second time, the finish improved considerably.

Even after my years of experience in restoring furniture and applying finishes things still go wrong. The only answer is to slap your wrist, strip it all off, and start all over again. Each time you re-do a finish you will learn something new. Do not settle for second best – this road leads to degradation and self-abuse each time you look at your unsatisfactory work.

Painting the interior

I gave the inside of the cupboard two coats of white undercoat, rubbing down between applications. At one stage I was quite taken with the combination of white and mahogany and was going to leave it at that. However, I soon realized that I admired the colour combination because it emanated a cool, classic feeling and that was the opposite of what I wanted. I mentally stored that idea for a future restoration.

I eventually opted for a bright yellow colour. I mixed just a few drops of bright yellow gloss paint into a white satin decorators' paint and stirred vigorously. I applied three coats of this, rubbing down between coats. The resulting effect served my intentions perfectly.

My brother was over the moon with the cabinet, especially when he opened it and revealed the yellow interior (quirky taste is genetic). His only regret was that I did not install a light that came on when you opened the cupboard, so that he didn't have to turn one on. After a few celebratory drinks, we decided that perhaps a clockwork mechanism that played a nursery rhyme would have also been a good idea. But that's what happens when you drink too much: such ideas are a salutary lesson for us all.

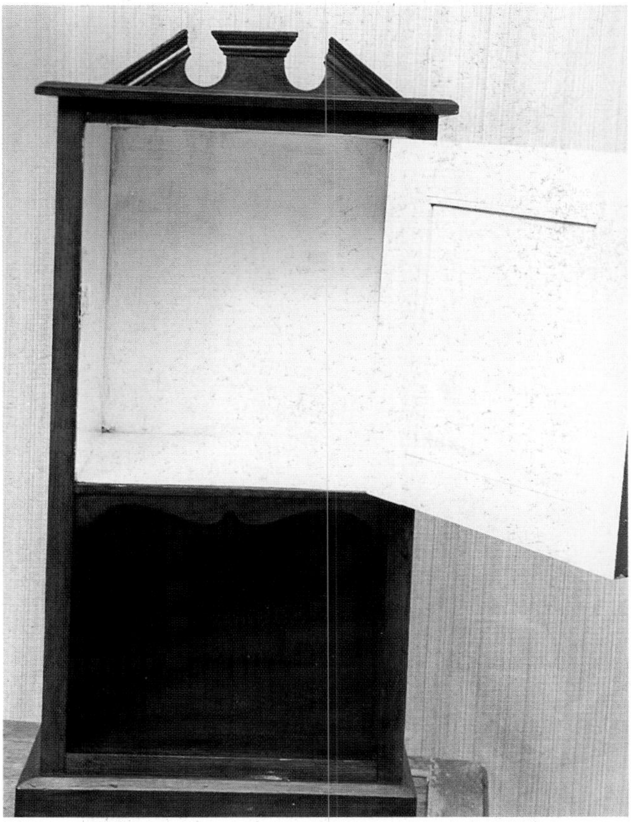

Fig 6.11 *The white undercoat.*

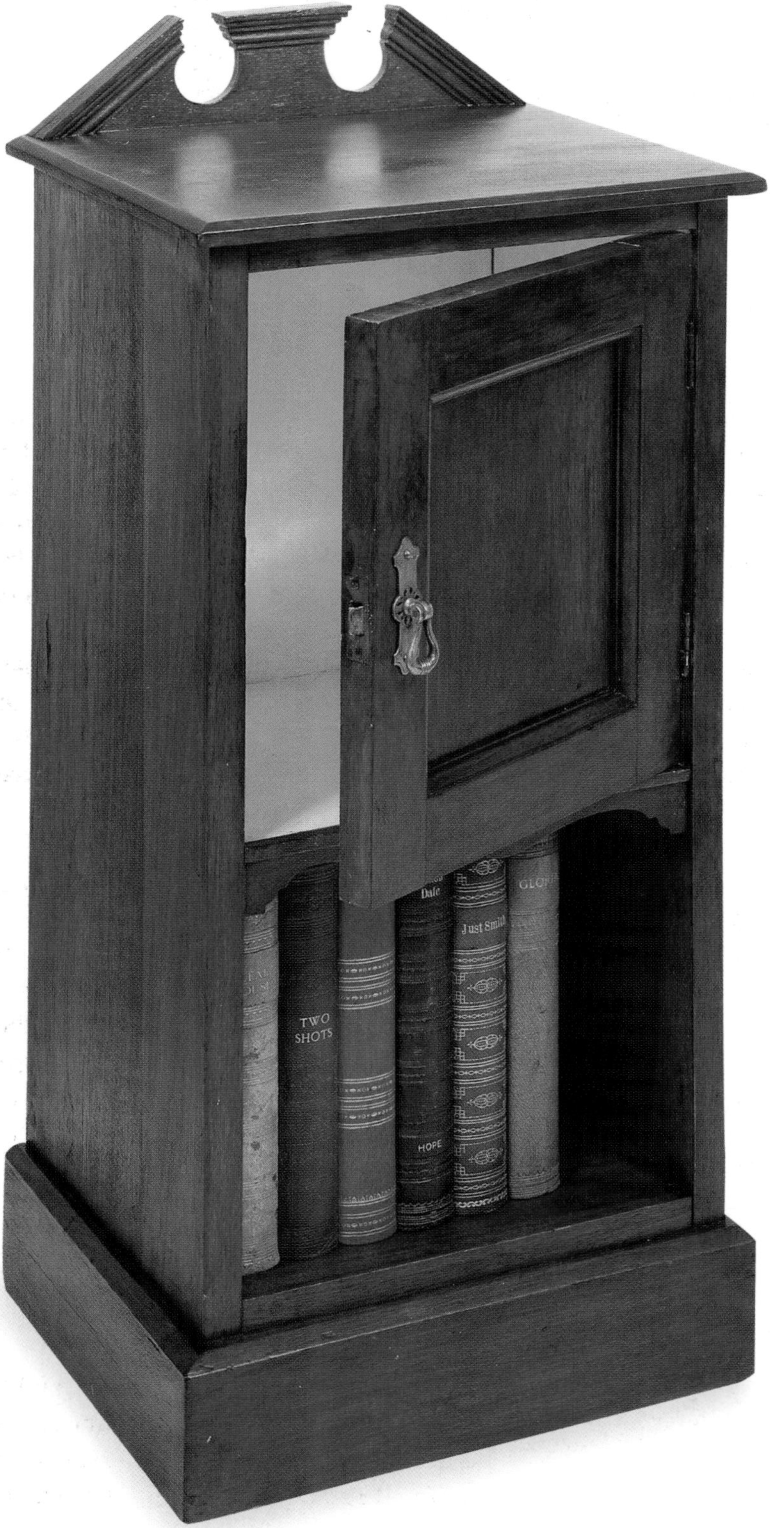

The restored cabinet put to use and, inset, in its unwanted state.

CHAPTER 7

Drop-Leaf Table

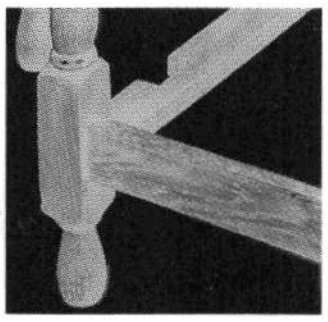

FINISH: POLYURETHANE VARNISH AND WAX

If you have any trouble finding furniture upon which to practise your craft, try this ploy. At the next social gathering you attend, casually drop into the conversation that you have taken up furniture restoration and you will be instantly swamped with enquiries after your services. It's always a great ice breaker.

That is how this restoration became tagged on to my ever-increasing list of things to do. I foolishly exclaimed that I was writing another book about restoring old furniture just before asking for another helping of Kath's Upside Down Chocolate Cake (which is a masterpiece of confection).

The hostess held the last piece of cake enticingly in mid-air with cruelty and cunning, before suggesting in an oversweet voice that she and her husband would be ever so grateful if I could restore their drop-leaf table. The request was accompanied by a withering look at her husband, who I later learnt had been promising for over 18 months to do the work. How could I refuse?

As soon as I agreed, the cake was slid onto my plate by the hostess, whilst the table was bundled into the back of my van by the much-relieved host. Well at least I won't starve.

Fig 7.1 *The much used table revealed.*

CONCERNING *Folding Furniture*

Furniture that folds down or changes into something else has always been in great demand. From the director's chair to the tilting pillar table and the occasional games table, this family displays some of the most ingenious work of furniture design. The drop-leaf table is one of the simplest and most common examples.

CONCERNING *This Table*

This piece of furniture is doubly useful because it is small and therefore easily transported around the flat when needed. Because it is so useful, it has received much wear over the years, witnessed by the deteriorated surface, the white marks caused by water and heat, and the black rings on the tabletop. When I was first shown the table, it was being hidden under a large tablecloth.

Apart from the necessary stripping and refinishing, one of the gate legs upon which the leaves of the tabletop rest is also suffering from old age; it needs dismantling, cleaning and regluing.

The table is definitely handmade. This is evident from the way some of the joints have been haphazardly cut. It was probably made some time between the wars. It is not a particularly refined piece of furniture, but the combination of English oak (from which it is made), practicality and handmade charm make it very attractive.

The Brief

The owners were quite insistent that the wood have a very natural look. No thick modern finishes or dark stains, but a natural, wholesome, light and clean finish. They suggested natural wax.

Wax is a beautiful finish, particularly on oak furniture. Along with oil finishes, a wax finish is one of the oldest known, requiring little skill to apply.

Hard beeswax can be softened by heating or the addition of turpentine. This enables the wax to be rubbed into the wood with greater ease and speed. More importantly for this piece, it will enable the wax to be brushed into areas that are difficult to reach, like the barley twist legs. When the turpentine evaporates, the hard wax is polished with a clean cloth. This process is repeated many times until the desired shine is forthcoming. A beautiful high gloss finish can be built up as the wax sinks deeper into the grain of the wood. Of course, over the years there have been one or two variations on this theme, but essentially the recipe and the process have remained the same.

As with all finishes there are problems. Before the turpentine evaporates, the wax is sticky and each application inevitably becomes ingrained with the dirt and dust of the day. This is one of the reasons why very old waxed furniture is black; it contains the soot from the open fires that used to be a part of daily life.

A second problem is that wax is not very hard-wearing; it becomes worn away through use, and damaged by heat and water. When this happens you have to apply another coat of polish to restore its good looks (much the same as the oil finish on the Fruit Bowl in Chapter 4).

This is not so bad on a sideboard or other furniture that is subjected to little wear, but this table is to be kept and used in the kitchen. With the amount of use it receives at the moment, it is going to need polishing at least once a week, if not more. This is unfeasible. Also, each application of wax will be accompanied by the smell of turpentine. On a food table, or in a food preparation area, this is not a good finish to use.

I explained all this while we finished the wine. These problems were definitely not to my hosts' liking. They wanted a wax finish but without all the attendant problems. A compromise was in order.

Adapted wax finish

Many craftspeople use an adapted wax finish that is intended to solve some of these problems and make the wax finish easier to live with. Before the wax is applied, the wood is sealed with a couple of thin coats of a hard finish. This has a number of benefits:

- the wax polish builds up a lot quicker so saving time and energy
- the sealer stops the wax sinking into the wood and thus keeps it on the surface, which stops the ingress of dirt into the grain of the wood
- the finish is harder wearing because the sealer, its foundation, is much harder and more resistant to scratching than wax.

In effect you get the toughness of a sealed finish with the beauty of a wax finish. Of course, there will always be people who argue that the traditional, more labour-intensive finish is superior to a sealed-then-waxed finish. The truth is, they are just different, to be used on different projects for different reasons.

You can buy ready-made sealers, though personally I think them an unnecessary addition to the workshop shelf; I prefer to make my own. The most commonly used sealer is a thinned french polish. This is used to seal the Chest of Drawers in Chapter 8. I used Danish oil as a final finish for the Country Chair in Chapter 5, but it can also be used as a sealer before waxing. Any finish can be used as long as it dries hard and is thin enough to soak into the wood rather than sit on the surface.

Because the table is going to be kept in the kitchen, used for hot dishes and subject to spilt gin and tonic, I decided against french polish as a sealer (french polish is damaged by heat and alcohol). Instead, I decided upon a clear, matt polyurethane varnish. It has no shine and little colour and is therefore visually inert just as I wanted. It is also hardwearing and resistant to water, scratches and the general abuse it would receive in the kitchen. Two thin coats of this should be sufficient to seal the wood, then I will apply a clear wax, rubbed in with wire wool.

The Plan of Action

1. Strip with chemical stripper.
2. Remove black rings from tabletop.
3. Fix wobbly gate legs.
4. Seal with two coats of polyurethane varnish.
5. Apply clear wax.

TOOLS AND MATERIALS

For This Table

(approx.)

- Chemical stripper, 500ml (18 fl oz)
- Methylated spirit, 400ml (14 fl oz)
- White spirit, 400ml (14 fl oz)
- Two-part filler, small 'splodge'
- Oil stain, 5ml (¼ fl oz)
- Beeswax, 250ml (9 fl oz)
- Polyurethane varnish, 250ml (9 fl oz)
- PVA glue, 10ml (⅖ fl oz)
- Large, flat scraper
- Wire wool
- Clean cloths, copious amounts
- Sharpened stick
- Broad stick
- Butter knife
- Sharp knife
- Pin
- Paint brush: 50mm (2in)
- Fine artists' brush
- Brush: 25mm (1in)
- Engineers' wire brush
- Boot polishing brush
- Fine grade sandpaper
- Chisel: 6mm (¼in)
- Soft-headed hammer

The Restoration

Stripping

As we experienced with the Bedside Cabinet in Chapter 6, you never know what you are going to uncover when you strip a piece of furniture. Sometimes there is a whole litany of problems waiting whilst at other times, as in this case, there is a beautiful piece of wood underneath the dross and gunge to brighten your day.

The top of the table was easy to strip. I used a chemical stripper and a large flat scraper to remove most of the old finish, then gave it another coat of thin stripper and attacked it with an engineers' wire brush (see Chapter 3). This is rough treatment, but I wanted to make sure that the open grain was thoroughly cleaned.

To my mind the beauty of English oak is in the coarse, open texture of the wood and the variety of grain and colour that the wood can display. In old furniture this is often obliterated by finishing with a thick, brown, glossy french polish. Scrubbing the tabletop with an engineers' wire brush restores the wood's natural qualities very effectively. The top took 45 minutes to strip.

My next task was stripping the legs. This is where my good luck left me. I sat for a good 30 minutes staring at the forest of legs and counted them over, and over. How can such a small and lovely table justify having eight legs? Each one of them needing careful and meticulous stripping. Such a task is where the beginner restorer usually comes to grief. Eight complicated, unremitting legs to be stripped.

I've said it before, but it needs saying again; the trick is to enjoy the work. Do not try and do everything at once. Do a little at a time. Prepare enjoyable breaks and look forward to returning to your labours.

I set a goal of stripping two legs before stopping for a break, and used the same technique as for the legs of the Country Chair in Chapter 5. I applied a thin layer of stripper, and after allowing it to do its work, I scrubbed the gunge with wire wool dipped in meths. The sharp recesses of the turnings I cleaned out with a sharpened stick (see Fig 7.2), and I finished off by scrubbing around the turned portions with a wire brush (see Fig 7.3). This operation uses a lot of meths and wire wool and is very messy, but it is effective.

Each of the eight legs took approximately 30 minutes to strip.

Fig 7.2 *Using a sharpened stick to clean out the recesses on the legs.*

Fig 7.3 *Scrubbing the turned portions with a wire brush.*

Removing the black rings

I scraped the three or four black rings on the tabletop using the same technique as for the Bedside Cabinet in Chapter 6.

This took no more than five minutes.

Filling the top

Using a wire brush on the tabletop exposed two small areas where the wood had been chipped. Although these blemishes are small, because of their location they demand an invisible mend. Any strange coloration, textural or other differences from the surrounding wood would attract the eye and encourage closer scrutiny.

I decided to use a two-part filler (see Chapter 3, page 15). If I were to use ordinary wood stopping, as I did to fill the knot hole in the Fruit Bowl (see Chapter 4), there would be a danger that it may fall out or crumble if somebody dropped a pot of marmalade on it. I needed something much stronger.

I mixed up a small quantity of filler with some hardener and pushed it into place with a butter knife. Because the top is a flat area, it

Fig 7.4 *Using a butter knife to fill the blemishes on the tabletop.*

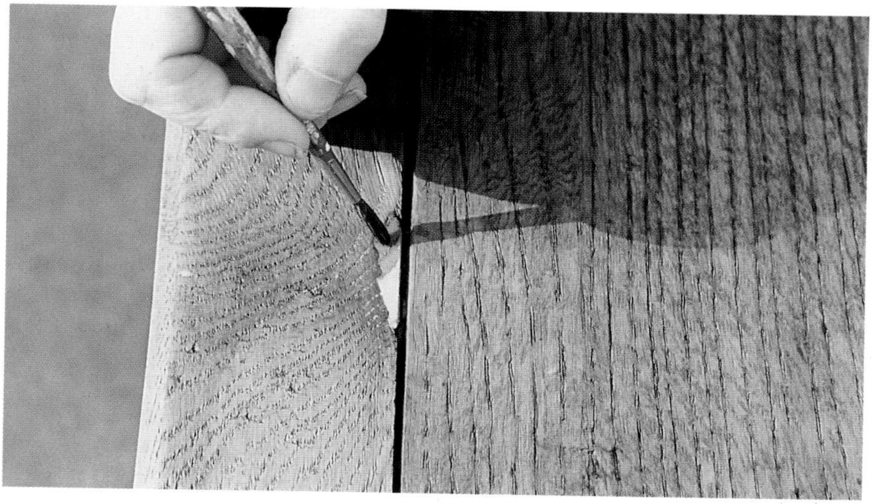

Fig 7.5 *Colouring the textured filler with oil stain, to match the wood.*

was quite easy for the filler to take the shape of the blemish, but it still needed sanding after it had dried to achieve a smooth finish.

Unfortunately oak is not a smooth wood. As we have already discussed, it has a texture. For an invisible mend, this texture had to be duplicated on the filler. I used a sharp knife and a pin to mark on a pattern, following the direction of the existing grain in the wood.

With the filler successfully textured, I applied the oil stain, to match the colour of the wood, with a fine artists' brush. The 'engraved' texture soaks up the colour, as can be seen in Fig 7.5. It takes a couple of applications before the correct colour is realized. I sealed the correct colour in with a drop of polyurethane varnish. The varnish had to dry overnight before I could apply any sealer to the tabletop, so I busied myself with fixing the gate leg.

Fixing the gate leg

The gate leg is the part of the table that swings out to support the drop leaf. The glued joints of this leg had come apart, making the section wobbly. This is a common fault in old furniture. To repair it, the joints have to be dismantled and all the old glue has to be removed, along with any other grit, before regluing and reassembling the leg.

I knocked the joints apart with a soft-headed hammer, then scraped the dowel joints with a sharp chisel to remove the old animal glue. I used a 6mm (¼in) chisel to scrape away the glue from the insides of the holes.

Scraping the joints took 20 minutes.

Golden Rule

The principle of removing all old glue before applying new glue is an important one. Glue cannot work unless it is in contact with the bare wood.

Tips

If you haven't got a soft-headed hammer to aid with dismantling, tape some cardboard to the part in question and use an ordinary hammer.

With the joints clean, I applied some PVA glue liberally and reassembled the gate leg. After a few minutes, I cleaned up any PVA glue around the joints with a damp cloth, and allowed the assembly to dry overnight. The joints were a tight fit, so I did not need the aid of any clamps.

Safety

Old animal glue can be glass hard. When scraping and chipping it can fly through the air. Protect your eyes and any other 'vulnerables'.

Fig 7.6 *Knocking the gate-leg joints apart with a soft-headed hammer.*

Fig 7.7 *Removing all the old glue by scraping with a sharp chisel.*

Fig 7.8 *Brushing on the sealer.*

Tips

Animal glue is heat- and water-soluble and can therefore be softened with a hot, damp cloth. Use this method prior to scraping off old glue if desired.

Applying sealer

I gave the table two thin coats of matt polyurethane varnish (see Chapter 3, page 11).

I stirred the can of varnish with a broad stick to mix the contents thoroughly, poured some into a glass jar, and thinned it to a watery consistency with some white spirit.

This I applied liberally to the wood using a 25mm (1in) brush, working methodically around the table. I left the sealer to soak in for five minutes, then wiped off any excess with a clean cotton cloth.

I applied a second coat after 45 minutes, and left this to harden overnight. The next day, I lightly sanded the whole table with fine grade sandpaper.

Fig 7.9 *Unadulterated, uncoloured beeswax.*

Fig 7.10 *Buffing the wax finish.*

Waxing

There is a bewildering variety of waxes on the DIY store shelf. Many of these are described in Chapter 3 (see page 11). The wax I used for this project was unadulterated, uncoloured beeswax. It is possible to make your own from beeswax but I usually buy mine ready-made from a DIY store.

A wax finish is idiotproof. Rub it on, leave it to dry, then rub it off. Repeat the process until you are happy with the finish, or too tired, or both.

To wax the flat tabletop, I used a clean cotton cloth to rub the buttery wax into the fibres of the wood. I left this for one hour for the turpentine to evaporate and the wax to harden, then buffed with another clean cloth.

For the legs I used a slightly different approach; I thinned the wax with white spirit to make a liquid paste and brushed this paste on with a 50mm (2in) paint brush. This made it a lot easier to get into the recesses and turnings on the legs. I left the legs to dry in the warm sun for an hour, then buffed them with a boot polishing brush and cotton cloths.

Fig 7.11 LEFT *Brushing the wax paste onto the legs.*

Fig 7.12 ABOVE *Using a boot polishing brush to buff the wax finish.*

The resulting table was difficult to return to the rightful owners. I explained my dilemma to them and the problem was solved by the promise of two portions of Kath's Chocolate Upside Down Cake. I said I wouldn't starve.

The natural look of the adapted wax finish compares well with the blemished surface of the unrestored piece.

CHAPTER 8

Chest of Drawers

FINISH: FRENCH POLISH STYLE AND WAX

This piece of furniture was donated to me along with the Bedside Cabinet in Chapter 6. I took the cabinet straight away as it was small enough to store in my workshop until ready for restoration. This piece was much larger, so my neighbour agreed to store it, until I was ready, in her outhouse.

When the time came, I arranged for my son Thomas and his friend to carry the chest round the corner from my neighbour's to my workshop, because it is very heavy.

Fig 8.1 *The poor condition of the chest of drawers before restoration.*

This was a mistake. Roused from my workbench by the commotion, I witnessed the upturned chest hurtling towards me along the garden path. It was being pushed like a toboggan by my two 'helpers'.

They said they found it a lot easier to slide the chest on its smooth, wooden top rather than carry it. I told them what I thought, using a number of well-known Anglo-Saxon expressions. Their defence was, 'It was old', and 'besides, you enjoy fixing damaged furniture don't you?'.

While I pored over the damage, they made their hasty escape.

CONCERNING *Chests of Drawers*

Perhaps the oldest type of furniture is the simple storage chest, also known as a trunk. In its earliest configuration it was literally hewn from a tree trunk, hence the name. A natural development, when craft skills evolved, was to compartmentalize the chest and fit drawers to separate the contents – the chest of drawers.

CONCERNING *This Chest of Drawers*

This particular example shares the same classical architectural styling as its sister piece in Chapter 6, but this has a lot more majesty. It appears that the architectural/classical styling fits the function and scale of this chest of drawers much better.

As with the Bedside Cabinet, it is well made and constructed from good quality, richly coloured mahogany.

This is a complex piece of furniture, and the more complex the project the more essential the action plan becomes. As usual, the first stage is to investigate your furniture fully, then compose your action plan carefully.

The drawers

First I removed all of the drawers to examine them. The bottom drawer is destined for intensive care. It just fell to pieces as I removed it from the carcase. (The carcase is the framework of a piece of furniture before any doors, drawers, plinths and other parts are fixed.) All of the joints had become unstuck and the drawer front had two nasty splits in it. The right-hand side of the drawer was in three pieces. The drawer slip had broken away and someone had tried to nail it back into place with a 2in (51mm) nail!

Although this sort of bodging is a common sight in old furniture, and should be frowned upon, the fact that this piece of wood has been nailed into place and not lost or discarded is extremely good luck. If that single, innocuous, nondescript scrap of wood was missing, I would probably have decided not to bother restoring this piece of furniture.

Consider the work involved. The whole side of the drawer would have had to be re-made. I would have had to buy a suitable piece of wood, plane it to the correct thickness, and cut it to size. This sized piece would then have needed a groove routed in the side in order to accept the base of the drawer. Then, most difficult of all, I would have had to copy, exactly, each of the dove-tail joints, by hand.

In short, to re-make this seemingly inconsequential scrap of wood would have doubled the amount and difficulty of work involved in the restoration of this chest.

Fig 8.2 *The two big splits in the drawer front.*

Golden Rule

The more complex a piece, the more considered the action plan should be. The last thing you want to do is invest blood, sweat and tears in a restoration only to find that you haven't the time, money or inclination to complete the project.

That is not so bad in itself, but imagine if I had not planned for it and had already spent two or three days stripping and staining, perhaps even invested money in some new drawer handles before discovering the work involved, and then decided to ditch the project. My misery would have been compounded many times over.

The second drawer from the bottom was not so bad. The only real problem was that the glue had failed, making the drawer joints loose. To fix this, the drawer needed knocking apart so that the joints could be scraped clean of old glue, and the drawer reassembled with fresh glue as was done for the Drop-Leaf Table in Chapter 7.

The smaller top drawers were solid but needed cleaning inside. A previous owner had spilt something sticky inside one drawer and all the fluff and drawer debris had stuck to this over the years.

The runners

With the drawers out, I can check the condition of the runners. The runners enable the drawer to slide in and out of the carcase with ease. The runner mechanism is composed of two parts: the runner itself and the bottom of the drawer side, which bears on the runner. Because of the friction between these two parts, the wood often wears away here, causing a groove in the runner and the drawer side. (See Fig 8.4.)

This is a very common fault in old chests. If it is badly worn, the runner mechanism will need replacing. This is work for a well-equipped and experienced cabinetmaker as it

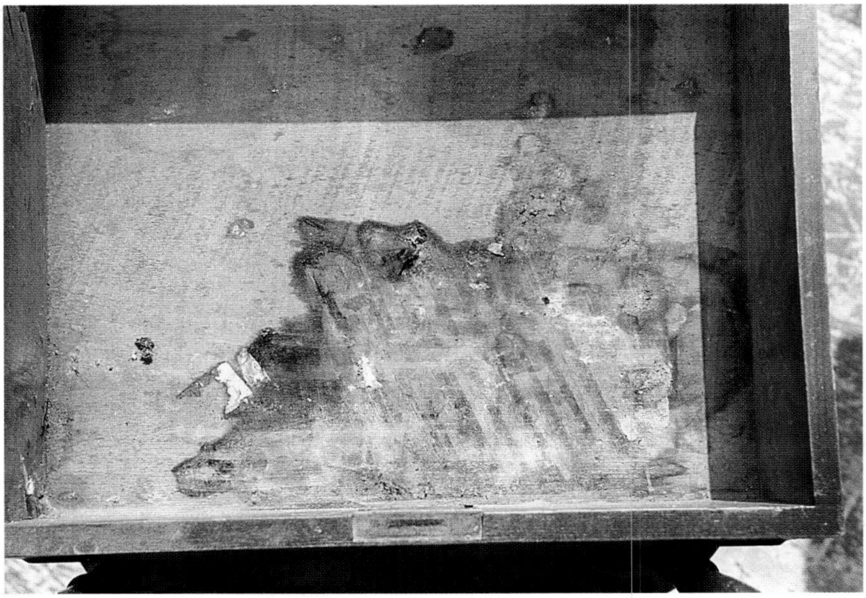

Fig 8.3 *The sticky stain and debris inside one of the top drawers.*

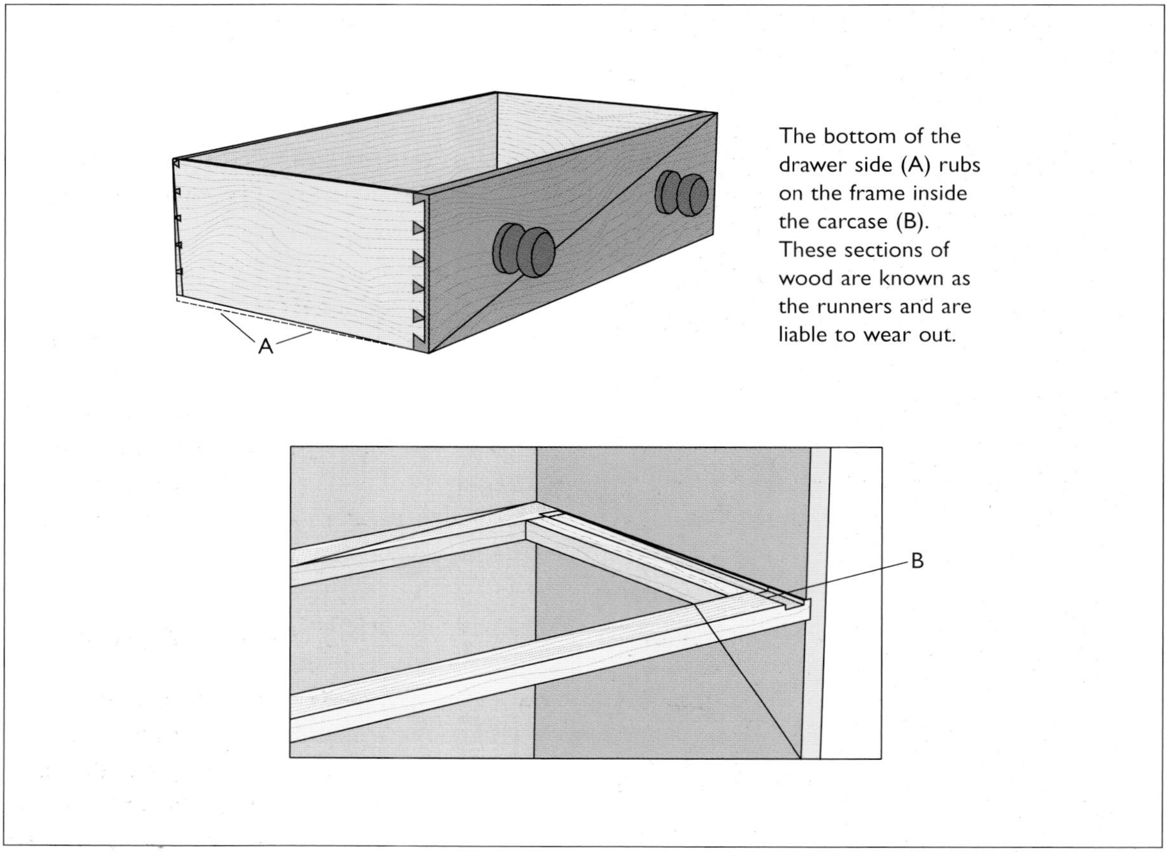

The bottom of the drawer side (A) rubs on the frame inside the carcase (B). These sections of wood are known as the runners and are liable to wear out.
A
B

Fig 8.4 *The runner mechanism.*

involves cutting out sections of the drawer side and replacing them with new wood.

If the runner mechanism does need replacing and you are not a cabinetmaker, don't bother restoring the chest; find another one to restore.

The drawer runners in this chest of drawers, although not perfect, were acceptable, so no work was needed.

The carcase

Often it is only the drawers that are stopping a carcase from falling apart. With the drawers removed, give the carcase a push at a top corner to see if it has any loose joints. If it is wobbly, you will have to dismantle the carcase, clean all the old glue from the joints, and reassemble after applying fresh glue. This process can be complicated and time-consuming. Luckily, in this case, the carcase was in very good condition.

While you are examining the carcase, look out for any woodworm or obvious amateur repairs. These are often hidden inside the cabinet where the inexperienced buyer/restorer fears to tread.

The drawer pulls

Often only one drawer pull will be missing or broken, as was the case here. This may seem like a small problem, but if you can't find a matching replacement, then you will have to

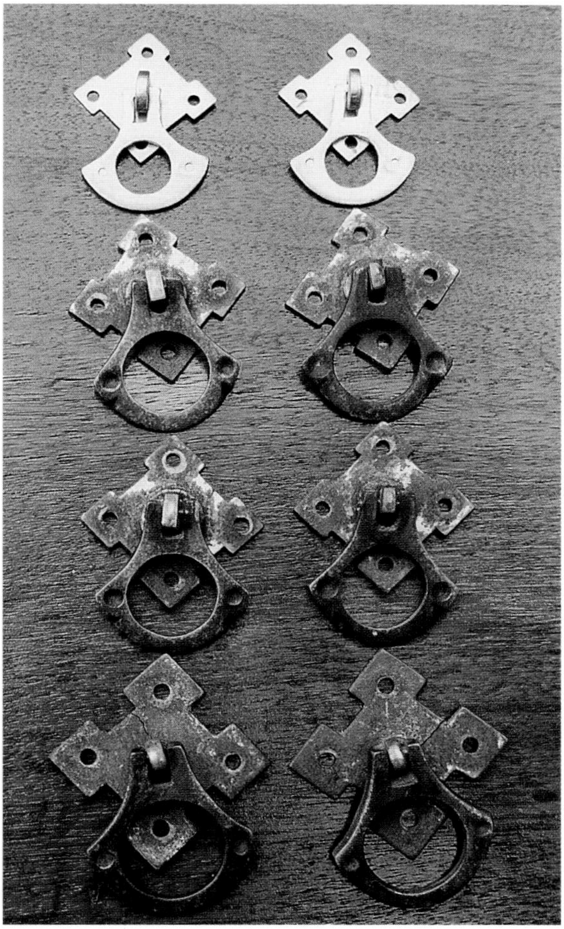

Fig 8.5 *The best match found for the drawer pulls; a smaller version of the same design.*

replace the full set. Brass pulls can be very expensive, so for large cabinets, which can need up to 10 pulls, replacing them all can be a costly business.

The top

The top was split in two places, one section had warped and lifted, and there were some deep gouges and scuff marks. It looked like some vandalous degenerate had turned the chest upside down and dragged it over concrete! Not to worry, I enjoy fixing this type of problem.

The Brief

This is a lovely and useful piece of mahogany furniture. I want to return it to its original condition. I intend to use traditional finishing methods. In this case there is no need to gild the lily – just allow its full natural beauty to shine through.

My teenage daughter, Joanna, has earmarked this chest for her bedroom and to this end has begun a campaign of verbal Chinese torture. This started with unsubtle hints that she hasn't got anywhere to store her clothes and will undoubtedly end in floods of tears and screaming and in my food being contaminated.

The Plan of Action

I have still not decided whether this piece is a viable proposition. There are a number of question marks over its feasibility remaining. Therefore, the first few jobs of the action plan are investigative; if they do not have a positive outcome, I may still abandon the project. My two-phased plan of action is as follows:

1. Research drawer pulls.
2. Repair bottom drawers.
3. Repair splits in top.

If the above jobs have a positive outcome, I shall go ahead with the project and continue with the following tasks.

4. Strip with chemical stripper.
5. Clean insides of drawers.
6. Repair dents and gouges in top.
7. Apply oil to make plaster invisible.
8. Seal with french polish.
9. Colour filled areas with spirit stain.
10. Apply coloured wax finish.
11. Attach drawer pulls.

TOOLS AND MATERIALS

For This Chest

(approx.)

- Chemical stripper, 500ml (18 fl oz)
- Methylated spirit, 500ml (18 fl oz)
- White spirit, 500ml (18 fl oz)
- Car body filler, 100ml (3½ fl oz)
- Linseed oil, 250ml (9 fl oz)
- Oil stain, 15ml (⅗ fl oz)
- Spirit stain, 5ml (⅕ fl oz)
- French polish, 200ml (7 fl oz)
- Wax, 100ml (3½ fl oz)
- PVA glue, 50ml (1¾ fl oz)
- Water
- F clamps
- Masking tape
- Wire wool
- Chisel: 6mm (¼in)
- Wire brush
- Paint brush
- Artists' brush
- Tissue paper
- Cotton cloths
- Screws
- Drawer pulls

The Restoration

Researching the drawer pulls

After a fruitless search through my collection of furniture hardware catalogues, I removed one of the drawer pulls and took it to Romanys in Camden to see if they had a match. Romanys is a well-known London supplier of furniture hardware and they have a comprehensive stock of old cabinetware.

Unfortunately, they only had a smaller version of the design. I considered changing all of the pulls for a different set, but that would have been well outside my budget. A cheaper option would be to replace the brass with wooden knobs, but this would most certainly look 'wrong'. Then inspiration struck; I decided to buy two of the smaller pulls and use them on the two smaller top drawers. This is not perfect but it is a pretty neat compromise in the circumstances.

Normally I would not buy the drawer pulls until the next two items on the action plan proved positive, but as they were the last ones in the shop and only 75p each, I decided to take the risk.

Repairing the bottom drawers

The drawer front

My next job was to fix the two nasty splits in the bottom drawer front. Unfortunately, at some time in the past, a misguided amateur had tried to fix the splits by squirting some glue into the cracks and hoping that would do the job. (This is a common bodge.)

Golden Rule

Do not be afraid to turn down a project if it is too expensive or time-consuming, or if you are not really interested in doing it. Sometimes it is better to cut your losses and run. Preferably, these decisions are made before you buy or have the piece delivered, but sometimes bad luck is the best teacher.

Fig 8.6 *Clamping the drawer front in position while the glue dries.*

Unless the split is now completely cleaned of all wax, dust and any other detritus, the glue will fail. This left me with the impossible task of cleaning out all of the naturally occurring dirt, *and* all the old glue that was located deep in the splits.

After much thought I composed myself, gritted my teeth and pulled tentatively and firmly at each split to break the bottom of the drawer front off completely.

Now that I had access to the faces of the split, I picked off the bodger's glue with the corner of a 6mm (¼in) chisel. I then soaked the unclean areas in white spirit and scrubbed them with a wire brush. (Remember, white spirit is the solvent for wax and grease.)

Once the white spirit had dried, I glued the bottom of the drawer front back on with PVA glue, securing it with five F clamps to hold it tightly in place while it dried overnight. I used masking tape to keep it from sliding about while I tightened the clamps.

The side panel

I then started work on the split side panel of the drawer. I removed the nail and glued the piece of wood back into place, securing it with masking tape while it dried.

There was still a large section of the drawer side missing. Luckily, this was just a plain piece of wood and could be replaced with car body filler. Car body filler is an exceptionally good wood filler. You can purchase a small tin of it from any car accessory shop, then just

Fig 8.7 *Replacing the missing wood with car body filler.*

follow the instructions on the can. The soft filler is made rock hard within minutes by adding a small quantity of the hardening paste which comes with the filler. Use it quickly before it goes too hard. You can build up very large sections of missing wood with this stuff, once you are experienced in its use. (For further information, see Chapters 4 and 7, pages 25 and 49.)

The car body filler will be coloured with an appropriate spirit stain later in the restoration process (see page 65).

The joints

The next day I scraped the old glue from the dovetail joints (this took approximately 20 minutes) and then reassembled the drawer. There was no need for clamps in this instance as the joints were tight.

When I had finished, I held my breath and slid the drawer carefully into the carcase; it worked just like new.

If the assembly of the drawer had been slightly wonky, if glue had been spilt on it, if the wood had swollen slightly, it may not have slid in so smoothly. In such a case, the drawer runners would have to be sanded or planed a little at a time to remove the offending parts.

I repeated the process on the second from bottom drawer. Again, this drawer did not need clamps.

Repairing the splits in the top

The solid wood top is made up from three pieces of wood glued together. One of these sections had started to warp, causing it to break away from its glue on the top of the carcase and split away from the rest of the top.

After some investigation and a number of experiments, which involved trying to glue the top from underneath with new glue blocks, I decided that the most secure way of fixing this would be to clamp, glue and then screw the top down.

Fig 8.8 *Scraping all the old glue from the joints.*

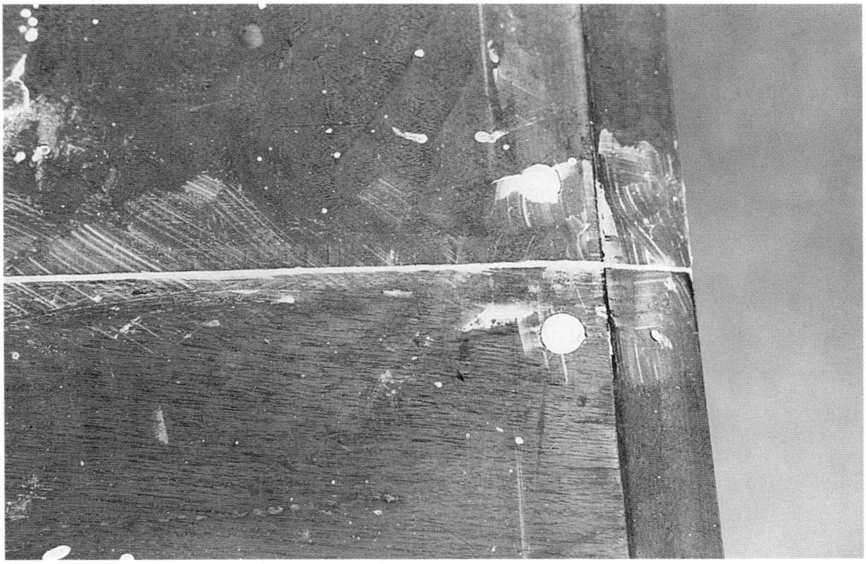

Fig 8.9 *The countersunk screw holes and gap between two of the wood pieces are filled with car body filler.*

Glue blocks are small, square sections of wood, typically 50 x 13 x 13mm (2 x ½ x ½in). They are glued along the intersection of two pieces of adjoining wood in order to join them together. They are commonly used on the interior, unseen portions of cabinets and often come unglued, thus weakening the structure. They can be replaced and would have pulled the top into place here, but I rejected this solution because in this instance they would not have been strong enough.

I drilled the screw holes so that the heads of the screws would be sunk below the surface of the wood, and then used car body filler to fill these countersunk holes. At the same time, I filled the thin gap that remained where the warped section of wood did not join exactly. I sanded down the areas of filler with wet and dry paper (600 grit), and shall stain the filler to match the surrounding timber after the cabinet has been stripped.

With the first three steps of my action plan successfully completed, I decided that the restoration *was* feasible, and so continued with the rest of the plan.

Stripping

Wherever there are structural jobs to be done on the furniture, it is best to leave any stripping until these have been successfully completed. There is an outside chance that the structural repairs will not be successful and you may decide not to continue with the restoration, in which case you will have avoided wasting time stripping the furniture. More importantly, structural repairs usually involve clamping and gluing, and glue will inevitably drip and splash. The old finish will protect the wood from contamination by the glue and will also help protect it against inadvertent knocks and marks caused by the clamps and other tools. Stripping the finish before gluing is a bit like laying a carpet before painting the ceiling.

I used a chemical stripper and followed the same technique as the one I used in Chapters 5, 6 and 7. Even though the work was mainly on flat surfaces, it should be noted that it took me a whole day to strip the chest. However, I didn't rush the job – it was quite a leisurely and pleasant experience.

Fig 8.10 *The surface of the wood after stripping.*

I started with the top, then moved onto the two sides before stripping the carcase front and the drawer fronts.

Cleaning the insides of the drawers

After stripping each of the drawer fronts, I cleaned inside each drawer by rubbing over with wire wool dipped in white spirit. Although they looked a lot better for this treatment, they will all benefit from lining paper and a spray of perfume. I shall leave this job to my daughter, who is now taking a very keen interest in the proceedings.

Repairing the dents and gouges

Dents and gouges are common problems and are easily removed. The repair relies on the principle that if water is applied to wood it causes the fibres to swell up or 'inflate'. When wood is knocked, the fibres of the wood are squashed or deflated; these can be re-inflated by the judicious application of water. This process is often referred to as 'raising the grain'.

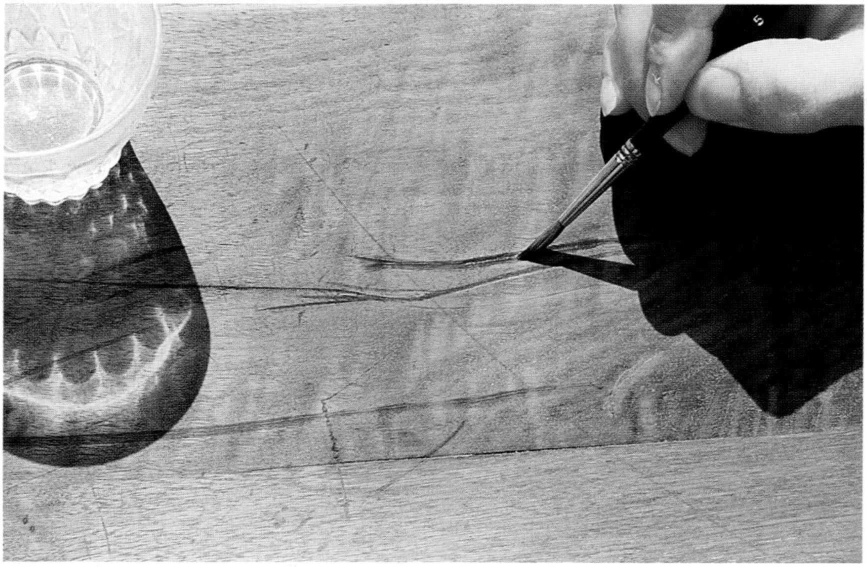

Fig 8.11 *Applying water to the minor dents to 're-inflate' the wood fibres.*

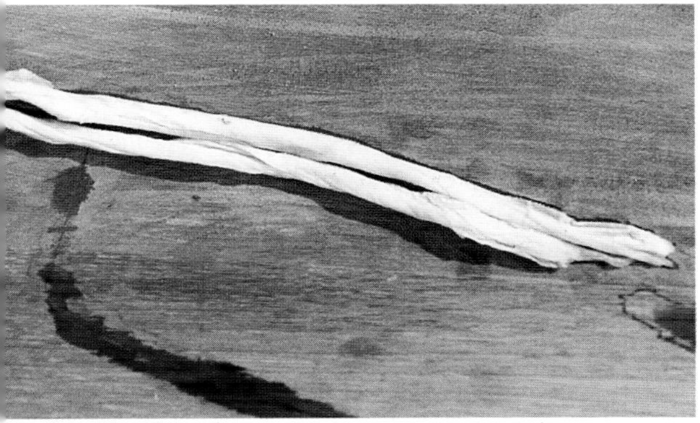

Fig 8.12 *'Snakes' of wet tissue are placed on the major dents and left overnight.*

For the minor dents, I simply painted on water with an artists' brush. As they dried, I applied more water, keeping the dents soaked all day long. By the end of the day most of the minor damage had disappeared.

I covered the more severe dents with wet tissue paper formed into snake shapes to follow the lines of the dents. In this way the dents can be kept wet for days on end if required. I left the snakes on overnight. By the morning the fibres had been re-inflated and the dents had disappeared.

In really severe cases, or if you are in a rush, you can apply the tip of a hot iron to the tissue, thereby forcing the moisture into the fibres of the wood.

Applying an oil stain

I obscured the plaster filler in the Bedside Cabinet (see Chapter 6, page 41) with oil stain. In this case I have decided to use a mixture of boiled linseed oil thinned with a little white spirit. To this I have added just a splash of brown oil stain to give it a little colour.

I brushed this mixture liberally onto the wood. In most areas the oil makes the plaster invisible immediately, but in a few stubborn areas, I needed to rub the oil into the plaster-filled grain with wire wool to get it to penetrate. Applying the stain took about 15 minutes. I left this for 10 minutes before applying a second coat to the absorbent areas, and finished by wiping off any excess with a cotton cloth.

Applying the french polish

For the Drop-Leaf Table in Chapter 7, I used polyurethane varnish as the sealer because of its protective qualities. For this project I intend to use button polish (a particular type of french polish) for the following reasons:

- it was the original finish of the cabinet
- it will impart a warm colour to the mahogany
- I intend to colour the various patches of filler with spirit stain.

Fig 8.13 *Applying the coloured oil stain.*

There is a very important relationship between spirit stain and french polish. The solvent for french polish and spirit stain is the same (methylated spirit): therefore, spirit stains can be used to tint and stain french polishes. More importantly, the stain can be painted onto the top of the french polish and it will adhere to the finish. It can then have further layers of french polish applied over the top, so capturing the colour between layers of finish. This method has been used by craftspeople to stunning effect in creating finishes, notably, to simulate different woods when 'matching and patching' furniture.

Having left the oil to dry overnight, I mixed equal quantities of methylated spirit and button polish, and brushed this mixture onto the wood. As usual, I systematically coated the chest one section at a time. The important thing to remember about french polish is that because it dries very quickly you have to apply it very quickly. Don't overload the brush; dip just the tip into the mixture and smooth it out before applying more polish.

I applied only one coat of this thinned button polish before preparing the stain to fill the coloured areas.

Colouring the filled areas

To colour the filled areas, I mixed some brown spirit stain powder with meths and added a splash of button polish. Using an artists' brush, I painted this stain over the car body filler in the drawer front, over the recessed screws and filling the split in the top.

If you have ever used watercolours, the process with spirit stain is very similar; you build up dark colours by applying many thin coats. This approach will give you close control over the process. If you do overdo it, the colour can be removed by rubbing with a very fine grade wire wool.

This is a time-proven system. The french polish sealer allows me to make mistakes. If I were to work directly onto the surface of the wood, the stain would soak directly into the fibres and be next to impossible to remove if I were to make a mistake. With a coat of the sealer applied to protect the wood, I can play around with colours and brush strokes until the cows come home.

Indeed, in this case I removed my handiwork twice because I was not satisfied with the look. (It usually takes a few attempts before you get the hang of it.)

Fig 8.14 *Painting on the coloured stain to conceal the car body filler.*

Once I had achieved a reasonable effect, I gave the stained areas a coat of the thinned button polish to seal the spirit stain. To finish, I then gave the whole cabinet another coat of button polish.

Within the two sealing coats of thin button polish we have entombed the colouring stain that obscures the filler. This will protect all of my painstaking artistry from future wear and tear, and from the wax polishing finish that is to follow.

Applying coloured wax

In Chapter 7 we learnt how to apply natural, uncoloured wax. Here we want to apply a dark wax to the chest. The idea is to try and darken the tone of the cabinet and to create a slightly older, more antique look by simulating a patina. This is a common subterfuge in antique circles.

On the DIY store's wax finish shelf you will find, along with natural, uncoloured wax, an array of coloured waxes. Don't bother purchasing these; make your own. To do this, scoop the required amount of natural wax into a screw-top jar, add a few drops of oil stain to taste and stir until well mixed. In this way you can create your own coloured or 'antique waxes' to suit your own needs.

Fig 8.15 *Mixing an oil stain and wax to create a coloured, 'antique' wax.*

Please note that you cannot mix spirit stain and wax; only oil stains and wax share the same solvent and therefore only oil stains and wax can be mixed.

I made some dark brown wax in this way and applied two coats following the same procedure as for the Drop-Leaf Table in Chapter 7 (see page 53). I rubbed the wax into the wood with cotton cloths, allowed the solvent to dry, and then polished the wax with a second, clean cotton cloth.

The dark wax builds up in the crevices and mouldings of the furniture and artificially replaces some of the patina that was lost in the stripping process.

Attaching the drawer pulls

Those of you with a perceptive nature will have noticed that the photograph of the finished piece shows different drawer pulls from those originally fitted. This is due to a small mishap that happened to befall me some while ago – Benjamin, my eldest son.

On finding my beautiful antique and irreplaceable brass drawer pulls stewing in an old tobacco tin filled with tomato ketchup (in order to clean them and give them a shine), he decided that they were obviously unwanted and threw them in the bin. In my frantic bid to find them, there followed much wailing and gnashing of teeth, not to mention swearing and the upturning of every corner of the house and workshop.

I eventually reconciled myself to the fact that they would have to be replaced. After a long search, I found an antique shop that was selling exactly the same brass pulls for £8 each! I decided to settle for these cheaper, inferior but nevertheless serviceable modern drawer pulls from a local DIY shop.

Needless to say, my son has been struck from my will which, if he carries on at this rate, will almost certainly be read 30 years too soon. This will serve him right because he'll receive nothing but debts, and a beautiful late-nineteenth-century chest of drawers with modern drawer pulls.

Once the new handles were in place, I asked my daughter, Joanna, to help me move the chest of drawers indoors. Always willing to lend a hand, she started to tip it onto its top.

'No problem,' she said. 'All you have to do is turn it upside down and slide it along the ground. I've seen Tom do it. It's much easier.'

The Chest of Drawers finished with the second choice of drawer pulls and, inset, the poor condition of the original piece.

CHAPTER 9

Coffee Table

FINISH: FRENCH POLISH APPLIED WITH A BRUSH

This project was rescued from the bonfire of another one of my neighbours. At first glance this project deserves to burn: all four legs are wobbly, the veneer around the rail is peeling, the top has a split and is covered with a disgusting plastic covering.

However, a closer inspection suggested that it might have possibilities, so I put it into the potting shed to await evaluation/restoration. At Christmas it was brought out, covered with a piece of cloth and used as a makeshift games table. During that short time it proved itself to be indispensable and, therefore, in need of immediate restoration.

CONCERNING *Coffee Tables*

To the novice this item may appear to be an antique; that was the intention of the person who designed it. However, it is not a fake or a reproduction; there is no fraud involved here. It is undoubtedly a twentieth century design.

It is what I call a pseudo-antique and takes its place alongside the Queen Anne TV cabinet and Chippendale filing cabinet – modern in manufacture, function and design, but with a style that belongs to earlier centuries.

When it was made, in the 1930s or 1940s, it was probably sold as being in the antique style. This type of styling is still prevalent today in much mass-produced furniture that alludes to the grandeur and value of antiquity.

A trip to any large furniture store will reveal low tables of a similar size. These may be given various names such as coffee table, lamp table, occasional table and even side table. The number of different types and styles of low tables of this size attests to their widespread popularity. Whatever its origin or name, this is a very useful piece of furniture that could find a place in any home.

CONCERNING *This Table*

The design and construction of this particular table is very simple. It has three main sections: a top, four legs and a circular rail.

Fig 9.1 *The coffee table as it came to me.*

The top is its most attractive feature – it is made from solid mahogany. A solid wooden top is always pleasant to find; it can wear the damage of many years and still look good. A chip here, a dent there; minor damage just improves its character.

The alternative sort of tabletop from this era is veneered plywood. Veneer does not carry the scars of age well and damaged veneer can be difficult to repair.

The four cabriole legs are made of beech. In its natural state beech is sand coloured, however, these legs have been stained brown to match the top – a common practice with cheaper furniture. At the top of each leg are two 'ears'. One of these 'ears' is loose and will need regluing.

The circular rail is my biggest worry. The construction is fine (it has been made by steam-bending thin strips of wood and gluing them together) but the outside face has been veneered to match the top, and herein lies the problem: this veneered facing is in very poor condition.

The Brief

Turn this piece of junk into a usable table, restoring its original type of finish and keeping its antique style.

The Plan of Action

1. Remove plastic covering.
2. Dismantle table.
3. Strip with chemical stripper.
4. Fix veneer on rail.
5. Fix cabriole leg 'ear'.
6. Reassemble table.
7. Fix tabletop.
8. Stain with spirit stain.
9. Finish with french polish.

TOOLS AND MATERIALS
For This Table
(approx.)

- Chemical stripper, 500ml (18 fl oz)
- Methylated spirit, 150ml (5¼ fl oz)
- Wood stopping, 10ml (⅖ fl oz)
- Spirit stain, 280ml (10 fl oz)
- French polish, 250ml (9 fl oz)
- Wax, spoonful
- PVA glue, eggcupful
- Masking tape
- Wide wallpaper stripper
- Chisel: 6mm (¼in)
- Chisel: 25mm (1in)
- Wire brush
- Brush: 50mm (2in)
- Wet and dry paper
- Wire wool
- Cotton cloths
- Screws
- Drum sander

The Restoration

Removing the plastic covering

Before anything else is done, that plastic has to be removed. Most people over a certain age have something from the 1960s they remember; some of them are pleasurable, some of them are ridiculous. This material comes into the second group, and for furniture restorers is a potent icon of 1960s bad taste – especially when it is used to obscure a fine piece of mahogany. One can only wonder what was in the water that

Fig 9.2 *Peeling off the plastic covering.*

caused such a widespread cultural myopia. On the strength of this one material, many furniture restorers confine a whole decade of cultural change into history's dustbin.

Alright! Alright! Maybe I am overdoing it, but it's my workshop and I am not doing any more work until the plastic has been removed.

On past occasions I have lifted the corner of this type of plastic with my fingernail, and peeled complete sections off in one go – this time it was more difficult. Because it was old, and perhaps because it was a cold day, the plastic was brittle so only small pieces could be peeled off before it tore. This became very tiresome very quickly and I resorted to scraping off the remaining plastic with a 25mm (1in) chisel. The whole operation took about 20 minutes.

It was whilst stripping the top that my heart sank. I was expecting the solid top to be slightly damaged. What I saw gave me a little more sympathy with the decision to cover the top with plastic. It looked like it had been used as a butchers' block: there were knife scars all over it. The mind boggles at how they got there. This will be very difficult to repair to any degree of respectability. In such intensive care cases, it is often best to obscure the tragedy under an ebonized or painted finish (see Chapters 11 and 13, pages 98 and 119). For now I shall delay my prognosis.

Dismantling the table

Originally the table was held together with animal glue and screws but the glue has become ineffective over the years due to age and dampness. When I removed all of the screws, the table separated into its three main components: top, legs and rail.

This has a number of benefits: in cold weather I can take the pieces inside to work upon them, and smaller sections are easier to work on at the bench; it provides access to the joints, which allows the old glue to be removed; and it makes storage a lot easier.

If the table hadn't come apart so easily, I would have tapped the joints gently with a rubber mallet. If this hadn't released them, I would simply have restored it in larger sections.

Fig 9.3 *Removing the screws in order to dismantle the table.*

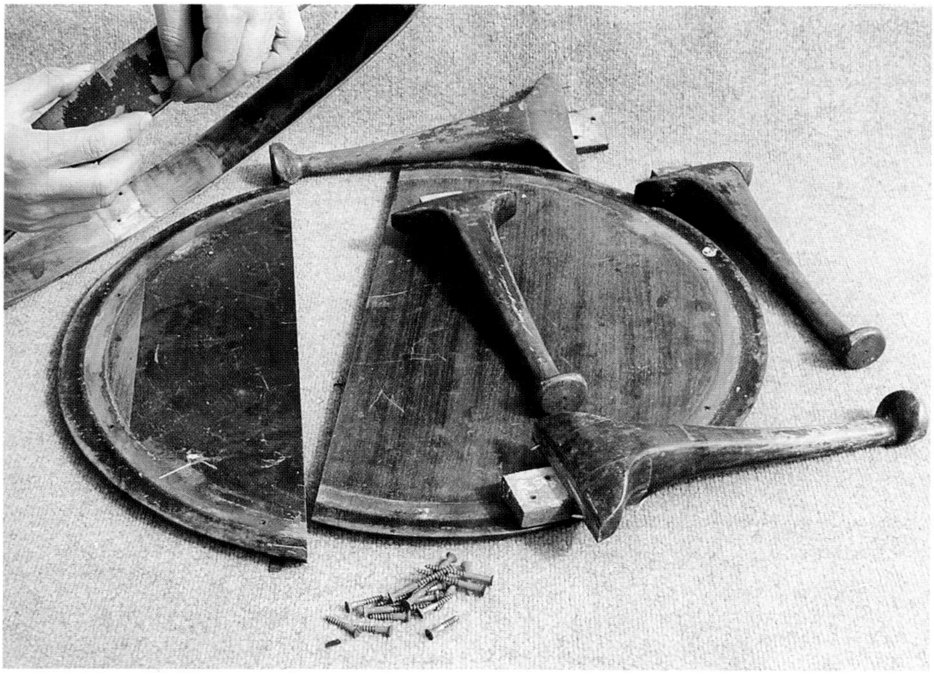

Fig 9.4 *The table components: top, legs and circular rail.*

Stripping

I used chemical stripper with a wire brush and a wide wallpaper stripper to remove the glue and old finish from the top (see page 28). This took approximately 45 minutes.

The legs I cleaned in a similar manner. I stripped as much gunge off as possible with the straight edge of an old chisel, then removed any remaining dissolved finish by wiping over the surface with wire wool dipped

Fig 9.5 *I used a wallpaper stripper and a wire brush to strip the top.*

Fig 9.6 *I needed a sharp chisel to get into the joints at the top of the legs.*

in meths. For the joints at the top of the legs, I used a sharp 6mm (¼in) chisel. The work on the legs took about 70 minutes.

Fixing the veneer

More than a quarter of the veneer has been lost over the years. The table has obviously been subject to a lot of damp. The glue has softened and the veneer has lifted and broken away. With so much of the original veneer missing, it would not be feasible to 'match and patch', or to stick down the lifted veneer as I did on the Bedside Cabinet in Chapter 6. This leaves me two options:

1. I could remove all the existing veneer and replace it with a completely new sheet; or
2. I could remove all the veneer and, if the wood underneath is of good enough quality, sand and stain so that the rail matches the top.

Much of the remaining veneer came off by hand; the rest required the use of a 25mm (1in) chisel to lever and scrape it off. It should be noted that veneer does not usually come off this easily. Normally it needs heating with a domestic iron to melt the old animal glue, after which it can be lifted off with a knife.

Once all of the veneer had been removed I cleaned the rail with a drum sander to remove any remaining particles.

The ground work was in very good condition. It is made from beech, the same wood as the legs. This is by coincidence rather than design, so it must mean I am having some good luck. Good luck is rare and should always be savoured.

With this find, I decided to follow the second option and stain the rail to match the top rather than replace the veneer. Staining will be a lot cheaper, easier and quicker.

Fixing the leg 'ear'

Due to its shape, the ear of the cabriole leg may be a difficult item to glue back into position. When it was originally made, animal glue was used. This type of old-fashioned glue made certain production jobs very easy. The joint was wiped over with a brushful of hot glue, then the ear was held in place for a few seconds until the glue cooled. With modern glues that need to be clamped, this sort of job is a little more difficult . . .

I tried PVA glue and a clamp, but the ear just kept slipping out of place. Finally, I bound the ear to the leg with masking tape while it dried overnight.

Fig 9.7 *I used masking tape to hold the ear in place while the glue dried.*

Reassembling the table

I attached the legs to the rail first, giving the joints an even coating of PVA glue before screwing the legs into place.

It was after all four legs were positioned and I was resting the tabletop in place, that I had my brain wave – why not turn the top upside down and display the clean, untouched, unlacerated underside?

By doing this, the only repair I need to make is to fill the eight screw holes with filler. This is chicken feed in comparison with the royal banquet of the other side, but most importantly, it means I can keep the original mahogany look. It's at times like this that you realize how wonderful life can be.

Fixing the tabletop

A split in a tabletop can be awkward to repair, especially if the top has bowed or twisted in any way, as they often do if they have been subject to damp. This is what had happened on the Chest of Drawers in Chapter 8. Luckily, this top was very flat which made fixing it a lot easier. All this good luck is making me uneasy.

I spent a little time with the table upside down, marking the screw holes. I also pencilled on a line to show where the rail would be positioned in relation to the tabletop before screwing the larger segment into place on the rail. With this in place, I applied glue to the edge of the larger segment then butted the smaller segment up against it, and finally screwed the smaller segment into place.

With the top refitted, I cleaned up the glue with a damp cloth and filled the redundant screw holes and a couple of small blemishes with wood stopping (see Chapter 3, page 14). The whole process took 45 minutes.

Staining

I often use an oil stain on a mahogany table, as I did with the Bedside Cabinet in Chapter 6.

Fig 9.8 *Repositioning the top.*

Fig 9.9 *Filling the screw holes with wood stopping.*

However, there is one small but very significant detail about this table that made me choose a spirit stain. Experience has taught me that those beech legs will not accept an oil stain very well.

After close-grained beech has been stripped, scraped and scrubbed, it often takes on a burnished sheen. This sheen tends to repel the oil stain and make the colour look weak and washed out. If you only need a slight colour change this is no problem. However, if ever I am working with beech and looking for a sharp colour change, I choose spirit stain. Spirit stain has a much stronger 'bite' which means it soaks into the wood a lot better than an oil stain, and overcomes the problem of 'burnished' beech.

Mahogany spirit stains can be bought ready-made from specialist suppliers. This can be misleading and annoying as there is no standard mahogany colour and 'Mahogany' could mean anything from a light brown to a deep red shade.

The colour that I associate with mahogany is a rich, dark red/brown. To get the colour of my liking I mix it myself. My mahogany recipe is 3 parts Spirit Brown powder (which is a chocolate brown) with 1 part Post Office Red powder (a tomato red) mixed with methylated spirit. For this piece I used 1½tsps of Spirit Brown with ½tsp of Post Office Red, and mixed this with approximately 280ml (½ pint) of meths. I added the meths a splash at a time, testing for colour as I went.

When the colour is satisfactory, I apply some of the stain to a scrap of wood. This allows me to check the colour and make any necessary further adjustments. I then apply the stain to the underside of the piece. This gives me one final chance to change the colour if it is not quite right.

I followed this procedure here, aiming to make the variously coloured sections all blend harmoniously together to look like one species of beautifully coloured, dark mahogany.

My carefully mixed stain, when tested on the underside of the table, obliterated any trace of wood and had a green tinge to the surface. This green tinge is a sign that the stain is too strong. I removed the excess by wiping over the surface with a rag dampened

Tips

Always mix the stain in a clear glass container so that you can hold it up to the sunlight to gauge its true colour. (This is a most important tip!)

with methylated spirit. By removing and applying in this manner, adding and subtracting, I can keep playing until I have achieved an agreeable, even colour.

All of this mixing, experimenting and staining (including my mistakes) took approximately 60 minutes.

Beware! No matter how hard I try to keep this stain under control it always gets all over my hands and clothes. Unless you want mahogany-coloured hands and matching trousers, wear gloves and old clothes.

Applying the french polish

Once the stain was in place, I mixed up a 50/50 blend of methylated spirit and french polish (see page 10).

To apply this mixture, I used the same brush that I used for the stain. The residue of stain in the bristles colours the polish, so adding to the depth of colour – and making the reason for cleaning the brush redundant.

Do not overload the brush. Dip just the tips of the brush into the mixture, and apply the polish with quick, even strokes and the minimum of brushing out. In the right conditions (warm and dry) the finish will dry very quickly. Just brush it on and move along.

I left the polish to dry for 30 minutes, then rubbed it down lightly with some 600 grit wet and dry, before applying a second coat. I gave it three coats, before leaving it to dry over-night in a warm, dry environment.

The next day I repeated the entire process. The more coats you apply, the shinier the finish becomes. Because the tabletop and the curves at the top of the cabriole legs will receive the most wear, and are also the focal points of the table, I gave them a few additional finishing sessions.

Once again, I left the table to dry overnight. I finished off with the remainder of the antique wax that I mixed for the mahogany Chest of Drawers in Chapter 8. This I rubbed in with a clean cotton cloth and left for an hour before buffing with a second clean cloth. It is worth buffing for as long as possible while the french polish is still slightly soft (within 48 hours). The abrasion of the cotton cloth will create a superlative shine.

Fig 9.10 *Rub the polish down between each coat.*

With the plastic covering (see inset) removed, the table is made respectable once more.

This is a little known variation on the french polishing technique of 'spiriting off' (more of this technique in Chapter 10).

The major problem with any french polish finish is that it can take up to a week to achieve its full hardness. Therefore, it is important that nothing be allowed to rest on the surface during this time.

Once it is fully hard, be sure not to spill alcohol on it or leave any water-filled vessel resting on its surface for too long: these things will also damage the finish.

CHAPTER 10

Side Table

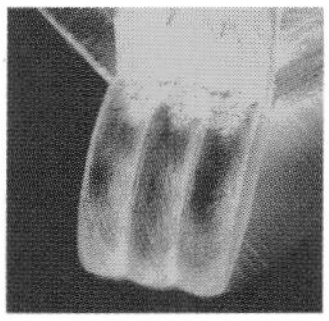

FINISH: TRADITIONAL FRENCH POLISH

This item belongs to my parents and has long been on my list of things to do. Each time I visit their house I am drawn to this table. I always promise as I leave that next time I get a chance I will restore it. Now, finally, I have the chance.

Many people take a sharp, deep intake of breath at the thought of french polishing – it has earned itself a reputation as a very complicated and highly skilled craft. However, as you are about to find out, restoring this table to glory with a traditional french polish finish is not as complicated as you might have been led to believe.

Fig 10.1 *The well-loved side table.*

CONCERNING *Side Tables*

Side tables like these are a common feature in junk shops and houses around the country. What never ceases to amaze me is how many different designs there are for this one, very functional piece of furniture.

CONCERNING *This Side Table*

This table is of very robust design. The legs are strengthened at floor level by a section of wood that has the same shape as the tabletop. I am sure there must be a specific name for this part of a table but I don't know it so I am going to call it the 'bottom shelf' for the purposes of this chapter.

Usually, side tables that have seen this amount of service and abuse are falling to pieces. This table hasn't even the merest hint of a wobble – a rare quality that should be cherished. However, its age is showing in the blemished finish.

I can't say that I find it the most beautiful of designs but would describe it more as 'interesting'. It was probably made some time between the wars. The top and the bottom shelf are veneered with English walnut, which is a beautiful and expensive timber used in the finest of furniture. The legs are made of the more commonly found beech.

The reeded legs and hint of a lion's paw at the base of the feet suggest that this table was inspired by ancient Egyptian culture. (Reeding is a decorative effect that resembles a bundle of canes or reeds tied together. Classical marble columns are reeded.)

I think it is this combination of solid construction with a rather subtle nod in the direction of Egyptian antiquity that makes the table interesting.

Furniture designers, in fact all of us, are influenced by the prevailing spirit of the age. In this way, certain pieces of furniture act as smoky windows through which we can peer into the past, revealing the influences and interests of the time.

In the 1920s and 1930s, every sphere of popular culture was fizzing with the new discoveries of western archeologists in Egypt. Songs were written, nightclubs were opened, films were made, books were written and clothes were designed, all in response to these discoveries.

Ultimately, even furniture design was influenced by the 'Egyptian look'. Perhaps this piece of furniture is an understated result of that time.

The Brief

Return this piece of furniture to its original condition, french polished and free from blemishes, ready to take on another 50 years of use and abuse.

The Plan of Action

1. Strip using antiquikstrip technique.
2. Remove ink stain.
3. Finish with french polish.

TOOLS AND MATERIALS

For This Table

(approx.)

- Bleach, eggcupful
- Chemical stripper, 500ml (18 fl oz)
- Methylated spirit, 300ml ($10\frac{1}{2}$ fl oz)
- Garnet polish, 250ml (9 fl oz)
- Wax, 75ml ($2\frac{1}{2}$ fl oz)
- Black marker pen
- Wire wool
- Cotton cloth
- Cotton wool

The Restoration

Stripping

In this project I am going to introduce you to a slightly different approach to stripping called antiquikstrip. This technique will only work on french-polished furniture, and should only be used on furniture that you intend to french polish again. It is one of the secret weapons of the french polisher and is often

Fig 10.2 *Beginning the antiquikstrip process.*

used on antiques. As the name suggests, it can be very quick.

We know from stripping the Fruit Bowl (see Chapter 4) that it is possible to remove french polish from wood merely by rubbing it with wire wool soaked in meths. Antiquikstrip is a variation on this technique. Instead of removing all of the finish, this technique removes just the top layers. If the finish is thick enough, you can remove all the layers that contain the scratches, white marks and discolourations with layers of polish still remaining. If the finish is thin, this will rub the polish back to the wood, leaving just a thin foundation coat of french polish in the fibres. Either way you will have a head start on the time-consuming and labour-intensive traditional french polishing process.

The beauty of this technique is manifold. If you are stripping or restoring 'antiques' with a french polish finish (and 90% of the furniture you encounter will have a french polish finish), you can leave part of the old finish on the furniture, thereby maintaining the original patina. Also, you can choose which parts of the finish you remove and which parts to leave alone. So, for example, you can antiquikstrip the damaged top of an old table but leave the comparatively well-kept legs undisturbed. In short, it is a very useful technique to have in your repertoire.

There is nothing like over-confidence to ruin a good plan. You can never guarantee that antiquikstripping is going to be successful and on this occasion it was not. I suppose if I had looked a bit closer (as I have been advising throughout this book) I could have seen what was coming.

The existing french polish finish was thick and should have been ideal for the antiquikstrip treatment. Unfortunately, it was so thick that over the years patches of it had flaked off. These are the lighter patches that you can see on the tabletop in Fig 10.1.

The antiquikstrip technique works by dissolving the existing french polish so that it becomes liquid and is redistributed over the surface by the scrubbing action, hopefully covering and correcting any blemish. However, the flaked patches on this tabletop were too large to compensate for in this way. Of course, this was not revealed until I had attempted to antiquikstrip.

There was also a problem with the black marks in the middle of the table, where black ink had been spilt. The alcohol-based ink had been left on the top for a very long time. This had dissolved the polish, allowing the ink to penetrate the fibres of the underlying veneer. Eventually the mess had been wiped up, leaving a deeply penetrating black stain in the grain of the veneer.

Antiquickstrip is good at removing light blemishes in the finish, such as water marks and surface ink stains that do not penetrate beyond the finish, and scratches, but these blemishes were far too extreme to be rectified in this way.

After a gallant 10 minutes of rubbing the surface with meths and wire wool, with fingers crossed, I saw the light and abandoned the technique in favour of the tried and tested chemical stripper. (See Chapter 5, page 28.)

This process took two hours.

Plan of Action After Stripping

And so my plan of action has been revised. (Do you notice a pattern developing here?) After stripping with chemical stripper I now need to:

1. Remove black stains from tabletop.
2. French polish using traditional methods.

Removing the black stains

Removing the finish solved the problem of the flaked patches, but not of the ink stains. I tried to remove them by scraping with a chisel (as described in Chapter 4, page 22). Again this had no effect. The stain was located too deep in the grain.

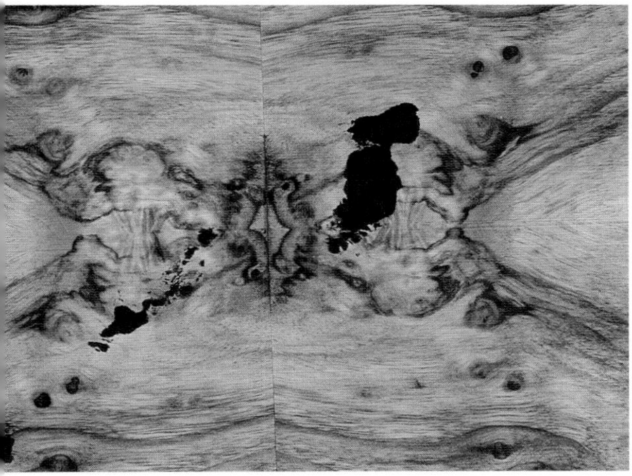

Fig 10.3 *The black stain penetrates deep into the grain of the veneer.*

There are a number of bleaching techniques and formulas available to the restorer. I am not a lover of bleach as I have rarely had a fun time with it, but in the absence of a better idea I thought I would give it a try.

Household bleaches can be used, but these are not very strong. I used a two-part proprietary wood bleach; specific wood bleaches are generally two-part. With these you apply the first chemical and leave it for 20 minutes before applying the second chemical. I completed this operation on three separate occasions with little effect, thereby reinforcing all my old feelings about bleach.

I considered other possible solutions, including cutting out the veneer and replacing it, or even cutting out the veneer, filling the

Fig 10.4 *Applying a two-part bleach in the hope of removing the black ink stains.*

crater and colouring the filling. I have employed both of these techniques on other furniture with excellent results, but they are last ditch options, to be used only when every other effort has failed.

At one stage I considered just leaving the stains and hoping no-one would notice. The walnut does have some very dark, almost black flashes of colour running through it, so the stain did not look *totally* out of place.

It was while pondering on this that I conceived a cunning plan. Sometimes it is best to hide your valuables in the most obvious places. Instead of removing the stain I would hide it amongst many other stains. I am sure there is an ancient oriental proverb that illustrates this principle perfectly, but how about this one?

> 'Sometimes it is better to hide your stain in a collection of stain rather than remove it completely.'

The veneer has been laid by quartering. This is a common method of laying veneers which relies on matching the pattern of grain configuration. Four consecutive sheets of veneer, which thus have the same figure pattern, are composed so that there is a mirror image running from left to right and from top to bottom.

Instead of trying to remove the stain I had the bright idea of reflecting the stain in the other sections of veneer, thus making the stain look like a natural feature of the wood. It may not be conventional but it's worth a try.

Whenever considering this sort of action you must ask yourself a most important question: 'Is the work I am proposing reversible?' If it is then carry on. You have nothing to lose and you will most certainly gain some knowledge if nothing else. If it is not reversible then think very hard, practise and experiment on an inconsequential piece of wood or furniture until you are certain it will be a success.

To start I brushed a thin coating of french polish onto the top to seal the surface. I then made a paper template of the stain by tracing over it with pencil and cutting the shape out.

I lined up the edges of the sheet of paper with the edges of veneer so that the template could be easily flipped onto the other quarters of veneer, and the shape of the stain traced onto them. On each quarter I filled in the shape with a black, spirit-based marker pen.

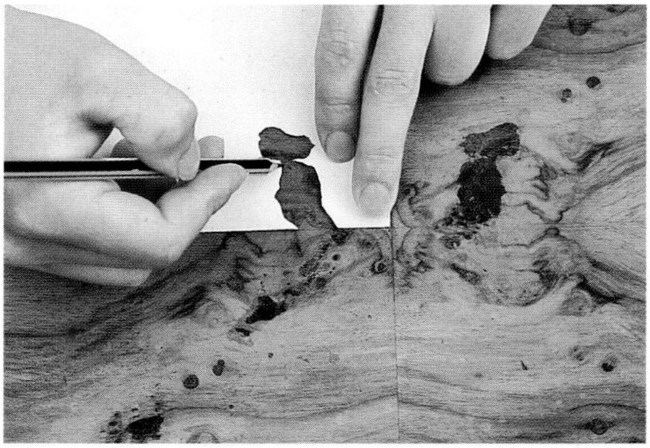

Fig 10.5 *The template is flipped into each quarter so that the shape of the stain can be traced.*

These new stains I then sealed in with a coat of french polish, applied with a brush. This sandwiched the spirit stain between two coats of sealer.

If I say so myself, I was very pleased with the results. A quick and simple answer to a knotty problem. I am sure that an experienced eye will look twice at the blemish and perhaps even uncover my subterfuge. In which case there is only one appropriate response . . . I shall lie through my teeth.

Applying the french polish

I used french polish as a sealer before applying wax to finish the Chest of Drawers in Chapter 8,

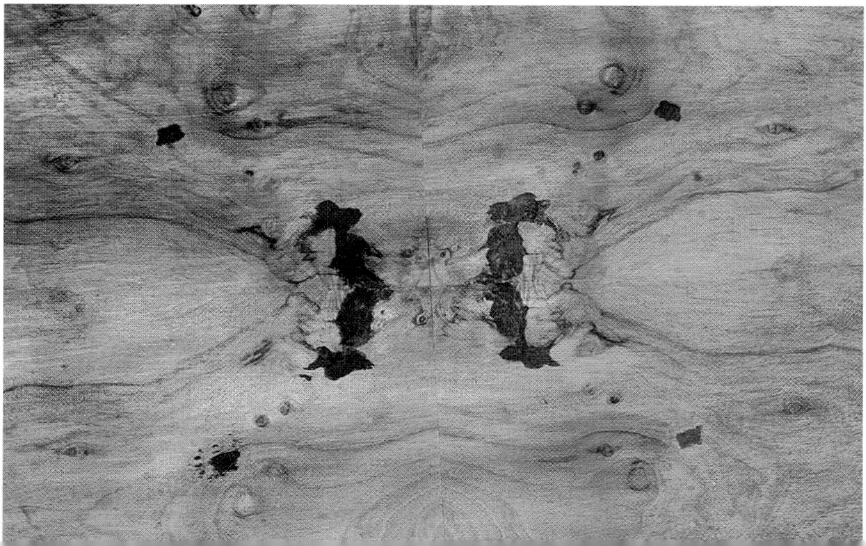

Fig 10.6 *The original stain hidden amongst my new stains.*

and applied french polish by brush to finish the Mahogany Coffee Table in Chapter 9. For this piece I shall follow the traditional french polishing technique of using a rubber to create a high gloss finish.

French polishing (the process of applying the liquid french polish to wood) was developed at the beginning of the nineteenth century. It was first used in France, hence the name, but soon spread to all corners of the world on its reputation. (For further information on french polish, the liquid, see Chapter 3, page 10.)

For traditional french polishing, the polish is applied not with a brush, but with a carefully constructed polishing cloth known as a rubber. This is made from cotton wool wrapped in cotton cloth (see Fig 10.8). The liquid polish is poured into the rubber and wiped over a section of the furniture leaving a very thin smear of polish on the wood. (This process is known as a pass.) Because this smear of polish is so thin, and because the polish has meths as a solvent, the coat of polish dries very quickly. By the time you have coated the furniture with one pass of the rubber, the polish where you first started is usually dry enough for you to start another pass. Many

Fig 10.7 *A traditional french polishing rubber.*

Tips

For making a rubber, you will find the folding a lot easier, and the whole thing will keep its shape without springing open, if you dampen the material in methylated spirit first.

hundreds of passes can be applied to build up a high gloss finish.

The process that I am going to use is carried out over three days. The first day's session is referred to 'bodying in' and lays down the foundations of the finish. Typically, the french polish soaks into the fibres of the wood overnight to provide a firm foundation for the second day's session, 'building up'. This is where the thickness of the polish is built up on the foundations of the previous application. This creates a finish that sits above the surface of the wood. The polish is applied in a number of passes, as for bodying in.

The third day's session is reserved for 'spiriting off'. No polish is applied. The existing semi-hard polish is burnished to a flawless high shine with a new rubber that contains nothing but meths.

Making a rubber

The rubber is the french polisher's secret weapon. They are constructed from pieces of cotton cloth folded around a large ball of cotton wool as shown in Figs 10.8.–10.15. They can vary in size from fingertip to palm size. For this side table I intend to use one about the size of a large egg, with the cotton pieces approximately 305mm (12in) square. I use curtain lining material for this (off-cuts are available at all good fabric shops).

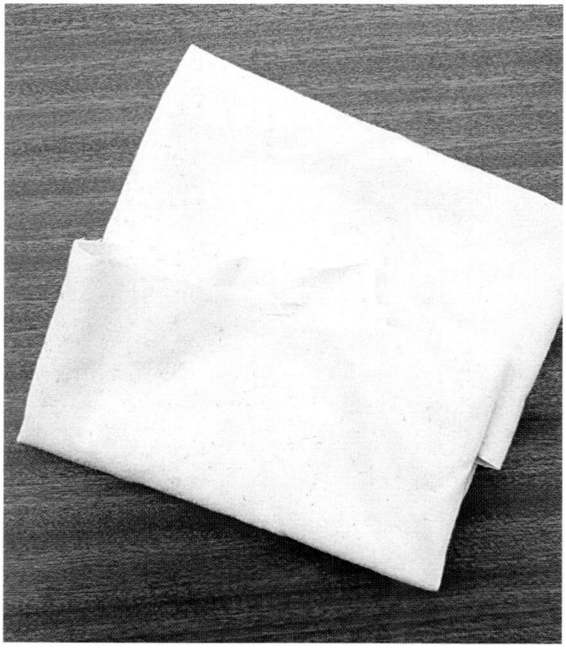

Fig 10.8 *Fold a piece of cotton material into a pad about 127mm (5in) square.*

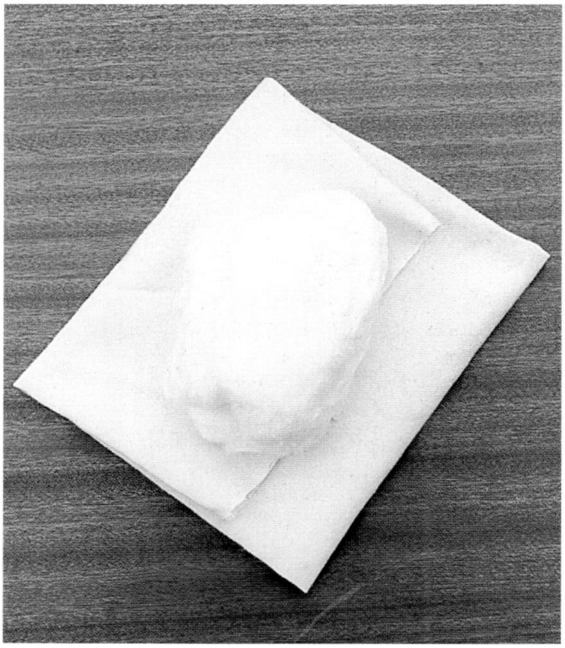

Fig 10.10 *Place the cotton wool in the middle of the cotton square and mould it into an egg shape.*

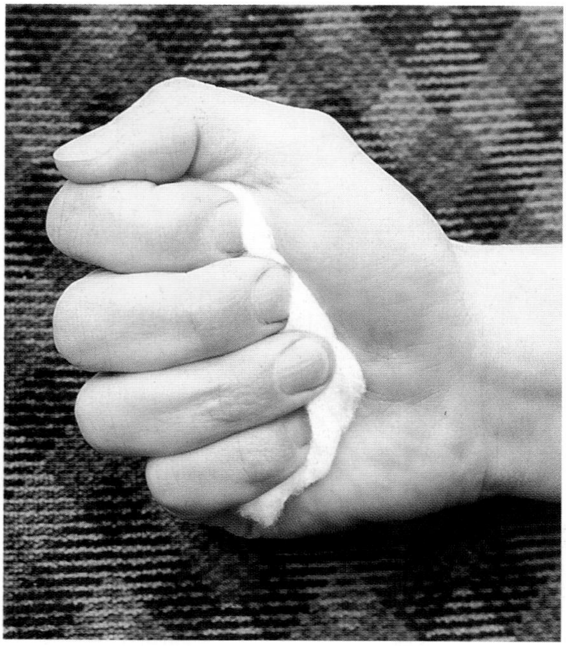

Fig 10.9 *Squeeze a large enough ball of cotton wool into your hand so your fingertips just touch your palm.*

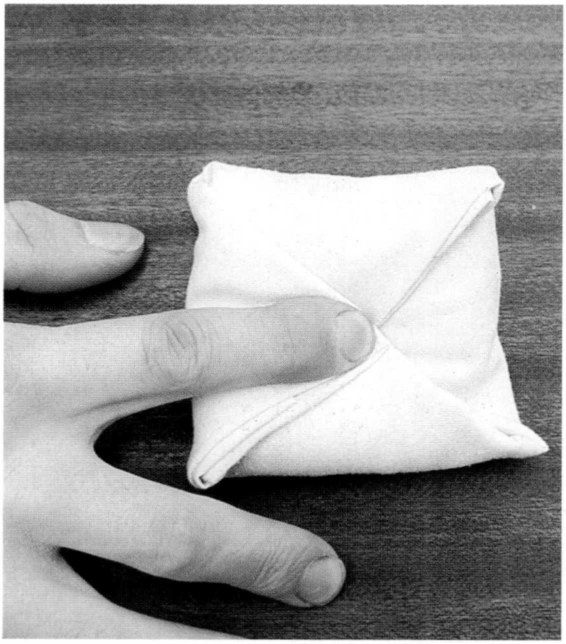

Fig 10.11 *Fold the corners of the cotton cloth over the cotton wool to form the 'fad'.*

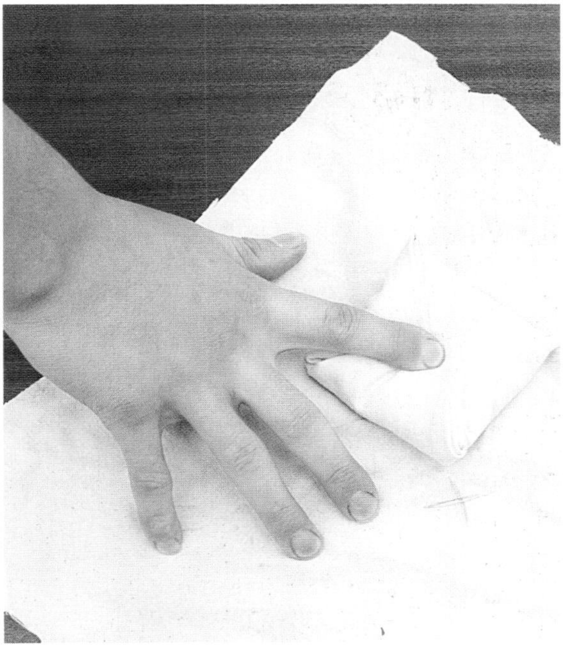

Fig 10.12 *Place the fad in the centre of another square of cotton cloth, then move it 25mm (1in) closer to a corner, as shown.*

Fig 10.13 *Pull the sides of the outer material up around the fad to cover it.*

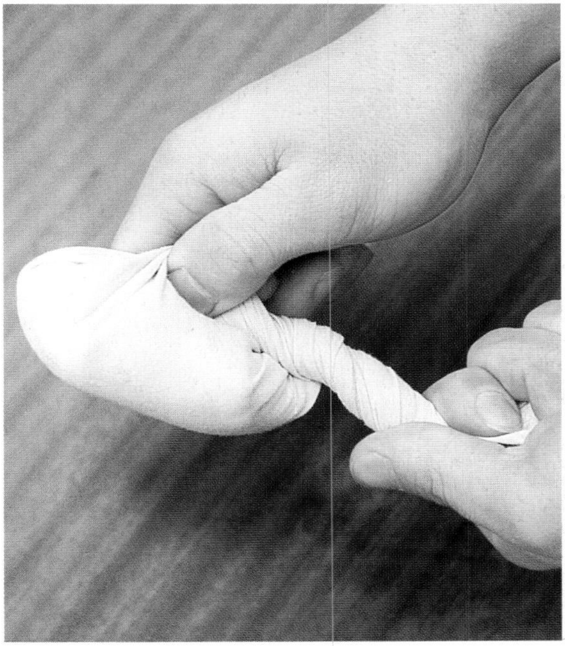

Fig 10.14 *Twist the loose material above the fad.*

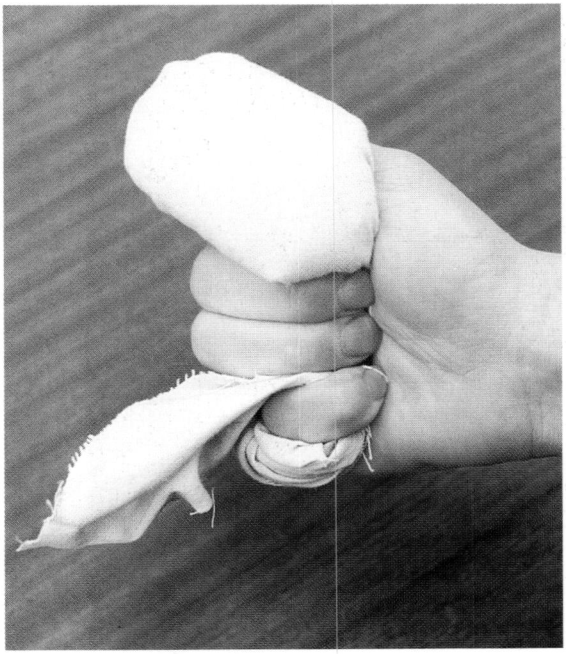

Fig 10.15 *You have now created a rubber, which should be held as shown here.*

If you have made the rubber properly it should be very firm to the touch, well packed with cotton wool, and with the cotton drawn up and tied very tightly so that there are no creases in the base of the rubber.

If you rub the rubber quickly over the palm of your hand, the friction caused by the texture of the cloth will warm your hand. It is this abrasive quality, constantly burnishing each layer of polish as it is applied, that creates the unique shine of a traditional french polish finish.

Charging a rubber

Now you must 'charge' your rubber with french polish. I used garnet polish, which is dark brown, for this table. (See Chapter 3, page 10, for information on other varieties of french polish.) This I thinned down with meths to a watery consistency. To charge the rubber I poured the mixture into the opened top so that it soaked the cotton wool interior, then wrapped the cotton wool up again and squeezed hard in order to push the polish through the bottom of the rubber. To distribute the polish evenly around the base of the rubber, I squeezed it down onto a piece of clean card. It took a few applications of polish to get the quantity right and the base of the rubber evenly coated.

Bodying in

With each french polishing job, you have to decide the order in which you are going to polish the parts of the furniture. In this case, I decided to polish the top, then the legs, and finally the bottom shelf.

There are three different passes that I use as shown in Fig 10.18. (Remember, a pass is a thin coating of polish applied with the rubber.) For the first pass, I start in the top left-hand corner and wipe the rubber from left to right in a straight line, following the grain of the wood. When I come to the right-hand

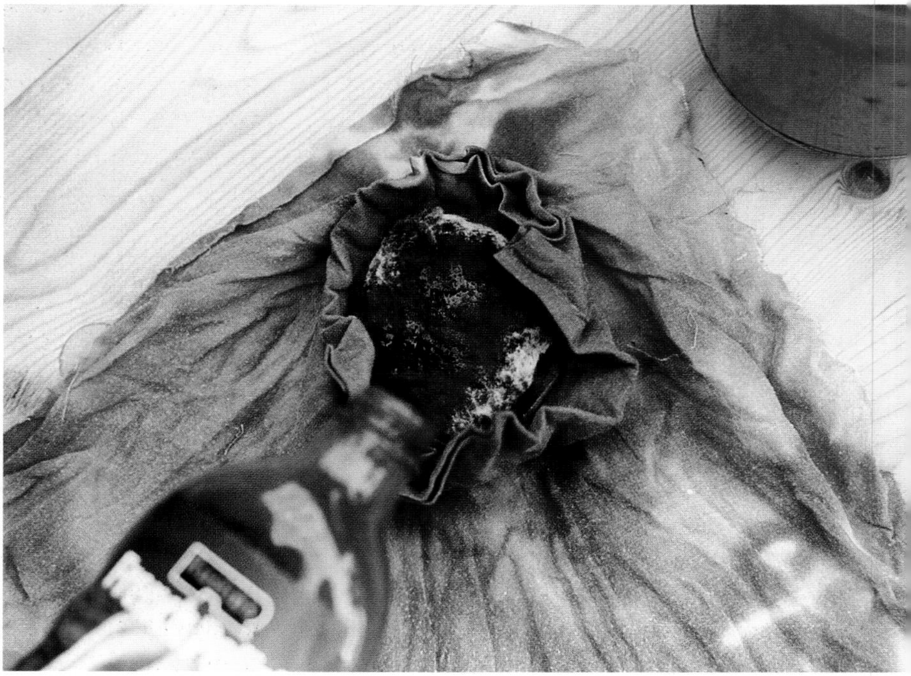

Fig 10.16 *Charging the rubber with polish.*

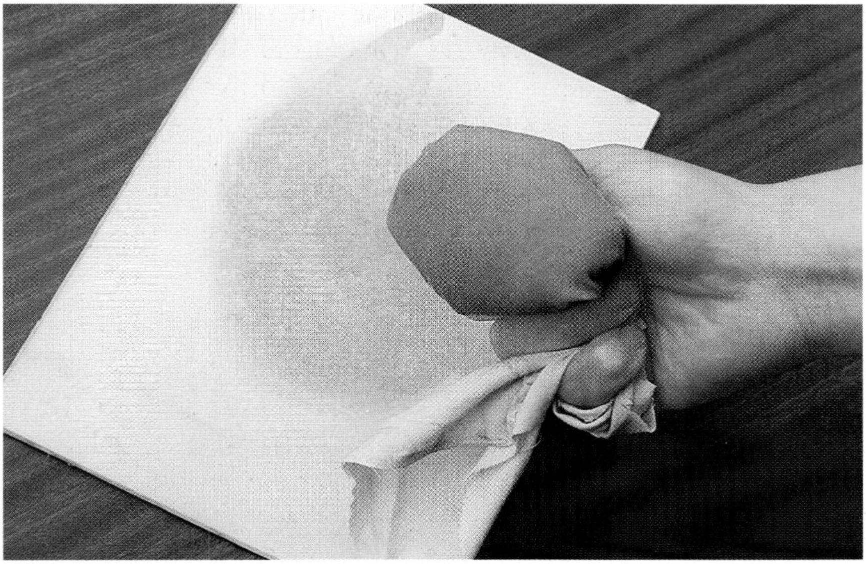

Fig 10.17 *The ideal quantity and distribution of polish on the rubber.*

corner, I lift the rubber off the wood and move it down a couple of inches to wipe in the opposite direction – from right to left. I work in the same pattern as a farmer would plough a field, wiping from side to side until the whole top has been covered.

I wipe on the second pass in the same way, except this time the passes are made working *across* the grain, moving from top to bottom until the whole surface has been coated.

For the third pass, I use small, circular polishing movements, again moving up and down the length and breadth of the tabletop.

This changing pattern of polish application ensures that the polish is evenly distributed and that no bits are missed, but more importantly, it guards against the polish building up a streaky quality which would occur if the same pattern was used to apply it for each pass.

The cardinal rule for the whole process is to always keep the rubber moving over the surface – never allow it to stop. If you do, the meths from the rubber will dissolve the hardened layers of french polish and cause the rubber to stick to the surface. As you pull the rubber to unstick it, you will create rough patches in the otherwise pristine surface.

If you do feel the rubber sticking to the surface, you must take evasive action. There are a number of possible solutions to this problem. Some advocate the traditional remedy of flicking raw linseed oil onto the surface. However, you can also speed up the motion of the rubber or lessen the downward pressure on the rubber, and improve your polishing action so that you do not slow down at those sticking points.

You should also avoid turning the rubber onto its side as you are polishing. The rubber is stickier on the top and sides because the polish exudes from these areas but does not get rubbed into the wood. It therefore remains on the rubber, thickens and dries out. This sticky polish can cause problems.

However, the simplest method, and the one that I advise my students to use, is to stop polishing for 30 minutes, allow the surface to harden a little and become less sticky, and then continue. Any or all of these actions can

Fig 10.18 *The three patterns of passes for flat surfaces.*

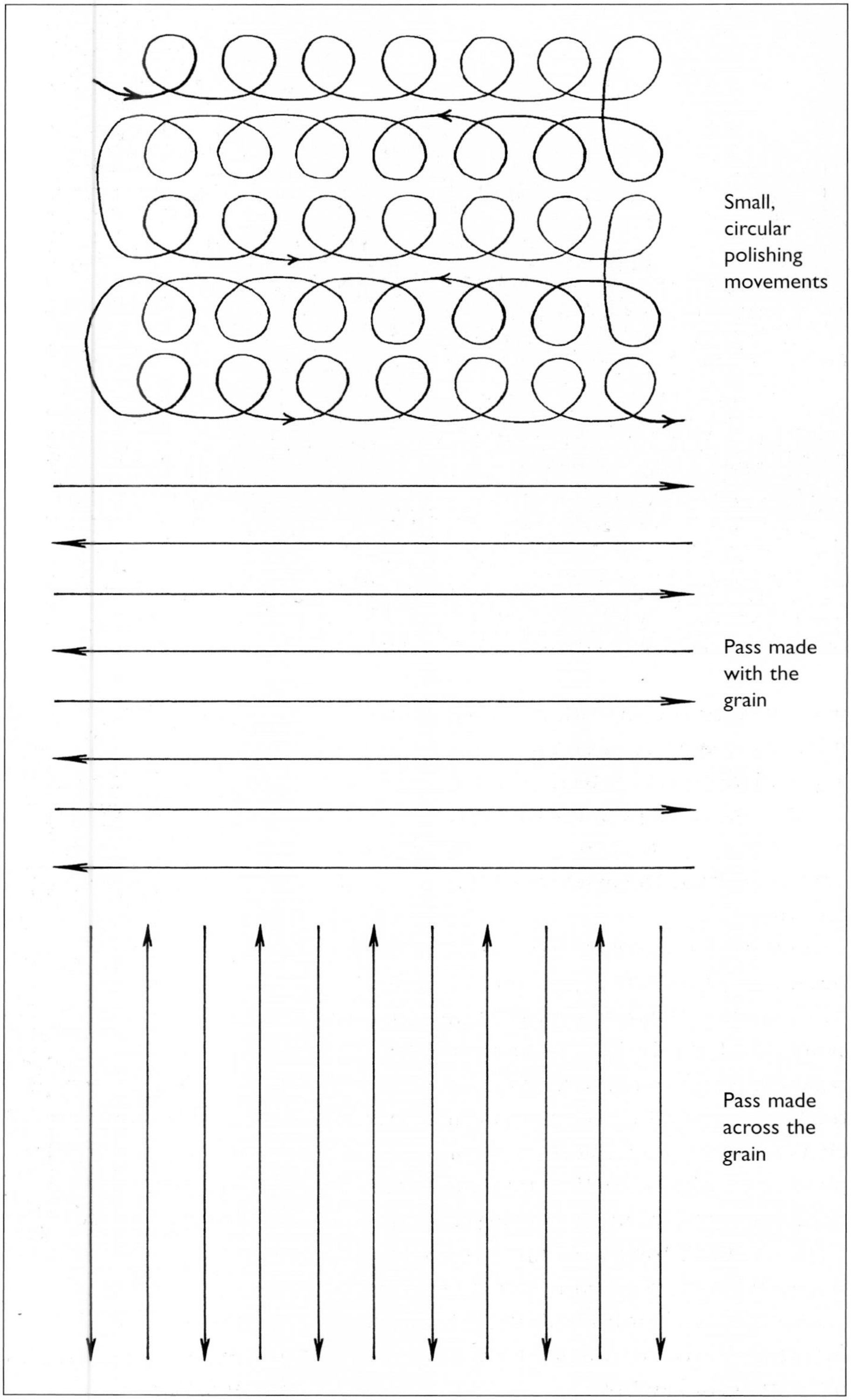

Fig 10.19 *Holding the rubber correctly for good contact with the surface of the wood.*

work; it is for you to work out where you might be going wrong and to employ the appropriate corrective technique.

After the third pass, I began again, repeating the cycle of three passes until I had applied perhaps 15 passes and built up a thick coat of polish.

I repeated the sequence of passes on the bottom shelf and the legs. It is not possible to be so particular with table legs because of their shape, but the principles remain the same. I wipe the polish over the length of the leg, then wipe across the width, and finish with circular passes of a fashion – as far as is possible. If I find areas that are difficult to reach, as in the reeding of the legs for this table, I scrunch the rubber up to the required shape and apply the polish with its tip. On another piece of furniture it might be more fitting to construct a smaller rubber for intricate work like this.

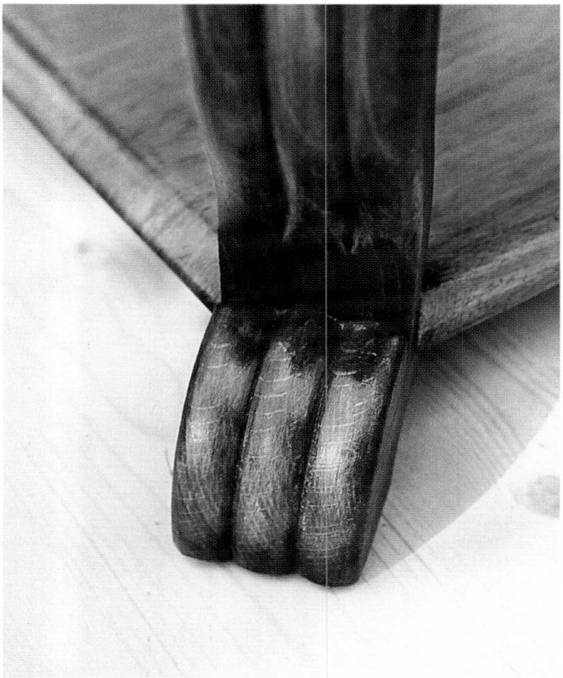

Fig 10.20 *I used the tip of the rubber to apply polish to the reeded legs.*

Once I had achieved a thick coating of french polish over the whole table, I stopped to allow it to dry overnight and soak into the fibres of the wood. (It is worth noting that this one day's work is acceptable as a finish.)

Building up

The next day the table had lost some of its sheen. This was because the polish had soaked into the fibres of the wood before it hardened overnight. I rubbed the table down lightly with wet and dry paper to remove any slight imperfections, and repeated the previous day's process to restore the shine.

By the end of the session I had applied another 15 or so passes and the polish was now raised above the surface of the wood. Again, I left this to harden overnight.

Spiriting off

Day three and the polish was ready for the final treatment – spiriting off. I made up a new rubber, charged it with methylated spirit and then rubbed it around the palm of my hand until the meths started to dry. It is important that the rubber isn't too wet at this stage.

Rubbing very lightly and very fast, I started to burnish the semi-hardened french polish on the tabletop. The polish is softened by the fumes of the meths, and the abrasive quality of the cotton burnishes the french polish to a superlative shine. I continued polishing in this way for 30 minutes.

This is the most rewarding and the most tiring part of the process. It can be addictive, so beware. In the past I have become so enthusiastic that I have rubbed all the french polish away, back to the bare wood, chasing that most seductive of surfaces – the high gloss french polish.

I finished off by applying a very thin coat of wax. This layer supplies a measure of protection against the natural enemies of french polish – water and heat.

This is just one account of how to apply a french polish finish. I estimate that there must be many dozens of methods that vary in detail and procedure. The important thing to remember is that the basic steps and principles are always the same:

- build up thin coats of polish
- apply the polish with a rubber
- use a variety of passes
- never allow the rubber to stop or stick to the surface
- spirit off with methylated spirit.

And, of course, get lots of practice.

Each method has its own batch of problems. Although the technique is neither the simplest nor the quickest, I have chosen it because, in my experience, it is the best technique from which to learn the principles of french polishing.

It is interesting to note that, on returning the table to my mother, the first thing she did was place a lace doily in the middle of the table, followed by a small vase of flowers, thus obscuring my painstaking work on the stain. She had not noticed the unique and decorative figure of the walnut veneer, but she was very impressed with the shine of the french polish and the reflection of the vase of flowers in it.

The traditional french polish finish has revitalized the badly blemished surface of this much used side table.

CHAPTER 11

Ebonized Dinner Table

FINISH: CELLULOSE LACQUER

Now this was a real find. This table had been dumped in the front garden of a local derelict house. I spotted some prime looking timber poking out of a pile of rubble and went to investigate. I often rescue odd bits of timber from skips and tips to store in my 'pile of wood that might one day be useful'. A closer inspection revealed that a whole table had been dumped. Not wanting the ignominy of rooting around rubbish tips, I went home and paid my youngest son, Samuel, and his friend 50p to do the dirty work.

They returned with a full-sized, oak, draw-leaf table which, considering it had been left out of doors for at least a couple of months, was in remarkably good condition. Later that week I spotted a similar table in a junk shop with a price ticket of £120.

CONCERNING *Draw-Leaf Tables*

This table is similar to the Drop-Leaf Table in Chapter 7 in that it is designed to extend when a bigger table is required and to 'shrink back' when not in use. The design stores the extension leaves under the central section of the table. This is a very common and effective construction method that has been utilized in a variety of table designs over the years, each one being solid and very functional.

CONCERNING *This Table*

The table consists of a large and heavy base that supports the three sections of the tabletop. The tabletop consists of one large, square, central section, under which are stored the two extension leaves that can be pulled out when needed.

All three tops are constructed from panels of 13mm (½in) plywood covered with an oak veneer. These panels have been framed with solid oak. This type of construction makes for a very strong, but light top.

If the tabletop had been made from solid timber, not only would it be very heavy, making it difficult to slide the outer leaves

Fig 11.1 *The dumped draw-leaf table.*

from under the central panel, it would also have been prone to splitting and twisting.

The base is also constructed from oak, except for some small pieces of beech that make up the bulbous turning on the columns. The whole table is finished with the standard inter-war finish of brown stain followed by a french polish.

The veneer at the corners and edges of the tabletop has surrendered to the elements; it has bubbled and is peeling.

Although all the old animal glue has been dissolved by rain, the table is still holding together through a combination of solid joinery and luck. There are some small sections of wood that have broken off, but most importantly, there are no major pieces missing.

In one respect the elements have worked to our advantage: the constant wetting, drying and wind has stripped the finish off one side of the table and the base. However, it has also caused the joints around the columns to open up and the wood to split. In short the table is a complete mess.

The Brief

I do not need a new dinner table nor do I know of anyone who needs a new dinner table. A sensible person would have resisted the temptation to take this table on board, but where's the fun in being sensible? Sometimes when fate throws something at you, you just have to catch it.

The truth is, this is an irresistible challenge. The curing of simple ailments have their satisfactions but there is nothing quite as invigorating as reviving the dead and buried. I know from past experience that if the restoration is successful it will plant a self-satisfied look on my face for many a day. And what better motivation is there than that?

Also, tables are a very desirable commodity, so I know that at some time in the future my work will be appreciated and put to good use.

However perverse my reasons for taking on this project, it does illustrate perfectly a principle that should never be ignored. Whatever projects you take on, no matter how essential, weird, wacky or useless they be, you must start the job determined to finish.

If you are not that bothered whether the project is successful or not, then as soon as you encounter the first problem (and I think by now we have established that problems are an integral part of the furniture restorers' craft) you will invent a plethora of very sane and reasonable excuses for turning your back on the work and giving up. You must be committed to seeing the work through or the job will never get done.

Because the table is in such poor condition, with many areas needing filling, I intend to obscure the resulting filled areas by ebonizing the table. Ebonizing is a technique which makes ordinary furniture made from ordinary timber look like expensive furniture made from the extraordinary, exotic, black ebony timber. The traditional technique includes emulating the very fine and particular texture of ebony, using age-old recipes, and finishing with a particular type of french polish finish. In years gone by ebonizing was a very highly skilled craft which employed many people. Such was the demand for their services, many craftspeople spent their working lives specializing in this one finish.

In recent years ebonizing, along with many other traditional techniques, has become debased. Today the term could be used to describe a piece of wood that has simply been stained black. Between these two extremes lies a continent of variation. What follows is just one of these variations.

In this project I am not really looking to trick anyone into thinking this is a real ebony table. My brief is simple – to make functional, attractive furniture from junk. Besides, because the legitimate ebony wood only comes in very small sections, furniture made from it tends to be of a lightweight and elegant nature. My cumbersome table would be a very poor starting point if I were to try and pull the wool over anybody's eyes. I am just trying to hide some of the necessary reconstructive surgery and give the table a suitably exotic air.

Ebonizing is a wonderfully easy technique. It is what I call a lifesaver finish. If all else fails, if the blemishes and stains and filler all become too much and you are finding it impossible to resuscitate your furniture, if you are about to give up – consider ebonizing. All manner of visual horror stories and 'creative' restoration can be hidden beneath the darkened cloak of the ebonized finish. It can obscure all traces of those impossible-to-remove stains or acres of filler. Most importantly, on the right type of furniture it can look very attractive.

The traditional Victorian recipe called for a smooth, close-grained wood. This was often beech, fruitwood or mahogany, but a number of other woods were used. The wood was stained with black spirit stain and finished with black french polish. The polish was applied with a rubber, but instead of spiriting off, it was rubbed back with fine steel wool and wax to give it a satin finish.

However, french polish is not the most durable of finishes and I would certainly not suggest it for a workaday dining table. For this reason I intend to forgo the pleasures of french polish in favour of a tried and tested recipe which uses black spirit stain and cellulose lacquer.

The Plan of Action

1 Rub back any loose, flaking finish on weathered part of table.
2 Strip tabletop with chemical stripper.
3 Repair veneer.
4 Fill grain of tabletop with plaster to obscure coarseness of grain.
5 Fill and 'rebuild' any split or damaged areas with car body filler.
6 Stain black with spirit stain.
7 Finish with cellulose lacquer.

TOOLS AND MATERIALS

For This Table

(approx.)

- Chemical stripper, 400ml (14 fl oz)
- Methylated spirit, 500ml (18 fl oz)
- Car body filler, 200ml (7 fl oz)
- Plaster of Paris, 300ml (10½ fl oz)
- Spirit stain, 15ml (½ fl oz)
- Wax, 75ml (2½ fl oz)
- Cellulose thinner, 250ml (9 fl oz)
- Water, 50ml (1½ fl oz)
- Satin cellulose lacquer, 500ml (18 fl oz)
- Craft knife
- Paint brush
- Medium grade sandpaper
- Wet and dry paper
- Wire wool
- Cotton cloths
- Socks
- Nails: 25mm (1in)
- Orbital sander

Fig 11.2 *One of the balusters on the table legs with the flaking finish stripped.*

The Restoration

Rubbing back

The first job is to rub back any of the loose, flaking finish that is still in place. Because part of the finish had already been stripped by the elements, most of the base needed just a gentle rub over with a medium grade sandpaper. The finish came off very easily in this way. I also used this opportunity to rub down any rough patches of wood. In total, this operation took about 30 minutes.

Stripping

The tabletop had been protected from the elements, so I am going to have to use chemical stripper to remove the finish here. I followed the same procedure as for the Country Chair in Chapter 5.

Repairing the veneer

Two corners of the tabletop had been damaged by damp. I cut away the damaged veneer with a craft knife to reveal that the plywood underneath had also been damaged,

Fig 11.3 *The bubbled and peeling veneer on the tabletop.*

Fig 11.4 *Cutting away any areas of damaged veneer and plywood.*

so I kept on cutting till I found solid wood, and filled the cut-out areas with copious amounts of car body filler.

It is worth noting that DIY shops sell a wood filler that is very similar to car body filler. I used this to repair the Drop-Leaf Table in Chapter 7. However, it is not as commonly available as car body filler and it is also often three times the price. So, when there is a lot of filler required, and it is to be obscured under dark stains or paint, I use car body filler. (See Chapter 8, page 61.)

Filling the grain

To emulate the very smooth and close-grained ebony wood, I am going to have to fill the

Fig 11.5 *Rubbing plaster into the grain.*

Fig 11.6 *I used an orbital sander to work over the large area of the tabletop.*

coarse grain of the oak wood with plaster. We encountered 'plaster in the grain' in the Bedside Cabinet and the Chest of Drawers in Chapters 6 and 8. However, in those pieces, the plaster was already in the grain and needed obscuring.

In this case, I am going to put the plaster in the grain. There are proprietary grain fillers that can be bought from most DIY shops, but the following technique is the traditional one, and also the cheapest. The process is quite simple.

You need two bowls. In one place some plaster of Paris (interior wall filling plaster will do), and in the other, a 50/50 mixture of water and meths. To apply the polish, I made a rubber from an old pair of socks, by stuffing one inside the other. This I dipped first into the liquid and then into the plaster, before rubbing it onto the wood, creating a slurry of plaster. This slurry is forced into the grain of the wood by the rubber. I finished off by wiping the rubber across the grain.

Once the plaster had dried, I started to rub over it with medium grade and then fine grade sandpaper, but I got fed up with this because the tabletop is such a large area. I finished off with an orbital sander. I also filled any smaller cracks and imperfections that I

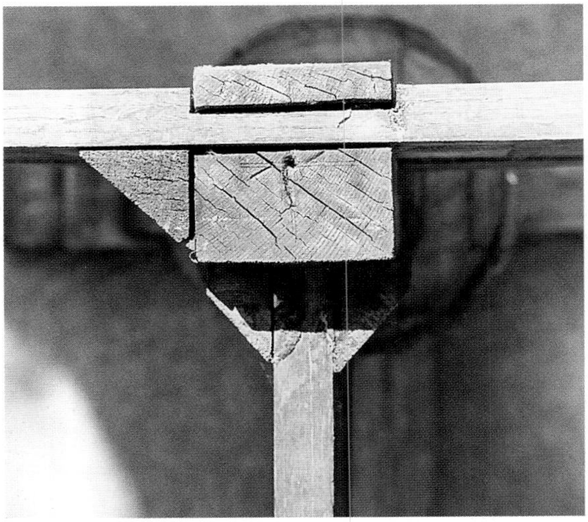

Fig 11.7 *Small cracks such as these should be filled with plaster, and sanded.*

found with the plaster mix, and again, sanded this down. However, I do not advise you to fill any large imperfections with this filler as it does not have much adhesion.

When the job is complete, the surface should be as smooth as marble – just like real ebony.

I repeated this process of filling and sanding on the other flat areas of the table.

Filling and rebuilding

The brackets under the frame of the tabletop have, in the past, become unstuck. These have been fixed back into place with a 50mm (2in) nail, and as a consequence, parts of the brackets have split off. These areas also need rebuilding, but for them I will use the stronger car body filler.

First I knocked some 25mm (1in) nails into the wood so that the filler would have something solid to bind to. I mixed up and applied a measure of car body filler to establish a very rough foundation for the shape, then built this up in a number of layers. Car body filler dries very hard, very quickly. After each application, I cut the filler back to the required shape with a sharp knife and coarse sandpaper before applying another mix of filler.

To obtain a smooth finish, I rubbed over the filler with a medium grade sandpaper.

Using this technique, a lot of patience, and a little imagination, you can build up whole sections of missing parts of furniture.

Each time I applied a layer of filler, there was a little left over, which I used to fill the other numerous cracks and gaps that I found. By the time I had finished, the table was solid, intact and very smooth.

Staining

I have described the use of spirit stain in Chapters 8 and 9 (see pages 66 and 74). My only new advice here is to ensure that you cover all of the table by turning it from top to bottom and side to side.

For the stain I added one teaspoon of black spirit stain to about 280ml (½ pint) of methylated spirit.

Fig 11.8 *Split areas such as these need rebuilding with car body filler.*

Fig 11.9 *Use a 50mm (2in) brush to apply the spirit stain.*

I stained all sections of the table, even underneath the tabletop. It is not often that I find myself under a table but when I do, I am often disappointed at the lack of attention to detail that is revealed. It only takes an extra few minutes to complete the job properly. If you are thinking of scrimping in this vital area, just consider the feelings of your guests when they have had one or two too many. After all, your reputation as a restorer relies on just this type of detail.

Spirit stain will dry very quickly in a warm, dry atmosphere and you can continue with the cellulose finish straight away.

Fig 11.10 *Apply stain to the whole table, including the underneath.*

Applying cellulose lacquer

Cellulose lacquer is one of the hardest, quickest-drying finishes available to the woodworker. It resists water, scratching and heat. It is, therefore, an ideal finish for furniture that is destined for hard wear or general abuse.

It is generally applied to mass-produced furniture in a factory situation, using an industrial spray gun. As such, it is not commonly available to the home woodworker. However, increasingly, manufacturers are producing varieties suitable for the DIY market. If you can't find one in your DIY store, don't give up; contact a trade supplier of woodfinishes. You should be able to find addresses in specialist magazines or in the phone book. Trade suppliers are wonderful places for the woodworker because they open up a whole new world of finishing supplies. Most of them operate a trade counter where you can go to obtain goods and drive the salespeople crazy with incessant questions.

Other manufacturers operate mail order schemes and are equally vulnerable to incessant questions, albeit over the telephone.

If your supplier sells the modern types of mass-produced lacquers, they should be able to supply you with specially prepared brushing formulas and all the attendant paraphernalia, like special brushes and cellulose thinners.

If you are restoring lots of furniture or large items, or are looking for a finish that will withstand everything that a young or abusive family can throw at it without complaint, then you should try cellulose lacquer or an equivalent modern lacquer finish. It is the ultimate in protection for your furniture and needs no maintenance.

The drawback with this type of finish is that the solvent is much more powerful, pungent and flammable than that in any of the finishes I have used so far in this book. You need to be a lot more careful with fire precautions, and you will certainly have to work outside when you use it, *and* wear a protective mask.

If you are still interested, here's how I coped. I poured some clear, satin cellulose lacquer into the same jar that I had used to apply the black spirit stain. Although the manufacturers don't recommend it, I have found that a small quantity of spirit stain will mix quite happily with cellulose finishes and tint the lacquer. I then added a few splashes of cellulose thinner until the mix was of a thin, watery consistency. This makes it easier to brush on the lacquer. If it is too thick, it will dry too quickly and, instead of flowing off the brush, it will become sticky and drag on the surface, leaving rough patches. This problem gets worse the hotter the weather is.

I brushed the finish onto the surface of the wood in the same way as I brushed the french polish onto the Mahogany Coffee Table in Chapter 9; very quickly, and without brushing

Tips

Do not be afraid to ask! I used to make it a rule to have at least three questions ready whenever I contacted suppliers. These people are the real chemical experts; they actually design and make the products that you are spending your hard-earned cash on. Do not waste this free resource. If you really want to know what the special additive they put into gloss varnish to make it matt is, or what the difference between button polish and garnet polish is, ask the question!

the area too much once the finish had been applied. It took approximately 30 minutes to give the table one coat of finish, including all of the normally unseen parts of the table.

I left the finish to dry for five minutes, then rubbed it very lightly with wet and dry paper to remove any imperfections. I then repeated the process, only this time I did not bother with the underneath, 'unseen' areas. Each time I applied a coat it became easier and quicker, as the finish flows better onto a smooth, non-absorbent surface than it does onto bare wood. Also, because it is easier to apply, there are less imperfections to be rubbed out with the wet and dry paper.

I applied three or four coats of finish to the base of the table, and seven or eight coats to the tabletop. I left this to dry hard over lunch.

Although the cellulose lacquer was supposed to create a 'satin' finish, it was too shiny for my liking, so I had to dull it down a bit by stroking the finish with a handful of medium grade wire wool dipped in wax.

If I had to do this job again, I would opt for a matt lacquer which could then be polished up a bit with clear wax. However, although rubbing back with wire wool is a little harder work, it probably has the same effect.

The final part of the process is to rub a little wax into the surface and polish it with some soft cotton cloths to remove any remaining soft wax from the surface.

Well, it wouldn't pass as ebony to the experienced eye, but even if I say it myself, I am very pleased with my find. A spare dining table for 50p – what a bargain. The only trouble now is that I can't pass a skip or a rubbish dump without scouring the rubbish for that elusive set of dining chairs to complete the set . . .

Fig 11.11 *Dulling down the lacquer finish by rubbing over with wire wool dipped in wax.*

The ebonized finish of the table obscures the areas of filling that were needed to restore the piece.

CHAPTER 12

Telephone Chair

FINISH: WATER-BASED, SATIN ACRYLIC LACQUER

Often a piece of furniture is destined to be placed in a particular environment. This chapter focuses on the problems this creates and the procedures that should be adopted.

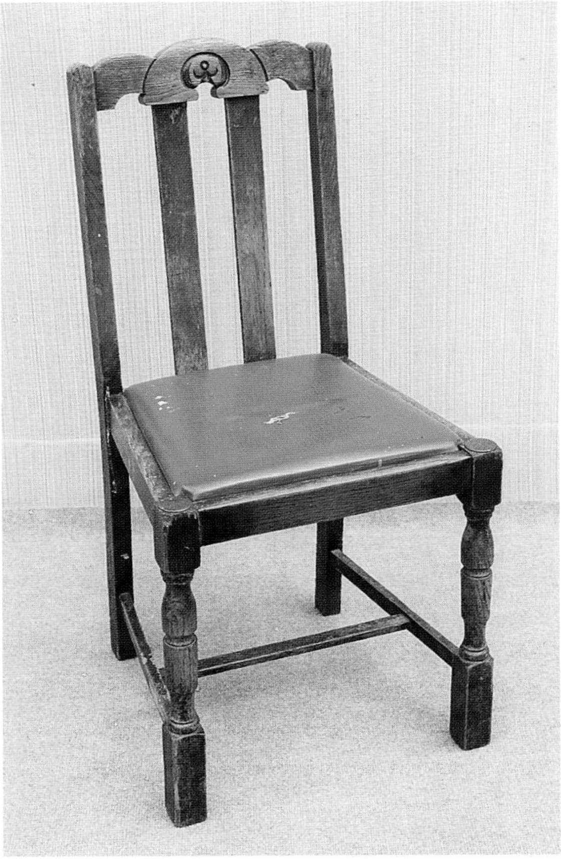

Fig 12.1 *The simple decoration on this chair makes a versatile piece.*

CONCERNING *Telephone Chairs*

This sort of chair is as common as trees in a forest. They can be found lurking around many homes, and can be bought for just a few pounds in almost every junk shop. Often, these chairs are the odd ones left, or separated from a set of chairs.

CONCERNING *This Chair*

Once upon a time this chair was part of a set of dining chairs. Alas, the other members of the set are long gone, making it redundant at the well-ordered dining table. This is a pity, as it is a very functional and hard-wearing chair, well worth the time and trouble of restoring to its former glory.

This particular chair has some interesting and appealing features. It is sturdily built, from English oak. The number of times this timber has already been encountered in this book reflects its popularity. In its natural state, English oak is a straw colour. However, in keeping with the fashion of the day, this chair has been stained dark brown and finished with french polish.

The style is quite simple, thereby lending itself to use in a modern, uncluttered setting.

Fig 12.2 *A beech frame, plywood board and wadding layer make up the seat.*

The only decoration is the simply turned front legs and the subtly shaped and carved top rail of the back. This is small cheese in comparison with the complicated ornamentation that can sometimes accompany this sort of chair.

The chair is fitted with a drop-in seat, which is covered with red imitation leather. This fabric has split over the years. The seat is constructed from a beech frame, with a thin board of plywood for support, cushioned with a layer of wadding. This is not standard. Most drop-in seats are more complicated – upholstered and with springs, webbing and wadding. The use of plywood in the seat suggests that the chair was intended for the cheaper end of the market.

The Brief

This chair is intended to fill a commission from my mother-in-law. She needs a chair to sit upon when using the telephone. In fact, she has been waiting for this chair for over three years, but this is the first chance I have had to get around to it.

I am not concerned with its antique qualities or its patina. This is to be a functional chair, for a particular job, in a particular place. I do not wish to spend too much time or money on the project, but it would be preferable to do a good job. Otherwise, come Christmas, I might end up with the wrong end of the turkey.

The Plan of Action

1. Examine intended room setting for chair.
2. Buy fabric for seat.
3. Strip with chemical stripper.
4. Re-cover drop-in seat.
5. Reglue loose joint.
6. Finish with satin acrylic lacquer.

TOOLS AND MATERIALS

For This Chair

(*approx.*)

- Chemical stripper, 300ml (10½ fl oz)
- PVA glue, 15ml (½ fl oz)
- Water-based, satin acrylic lacquer, 300ml (10½ fl oz)
- Yellow paint, ½tsp
- White paint, 50ml (2 fl oz)
- Fabric, 508 x 508mm (20 x 20in)
- Wadding, 508 x 508mm (20 x 20in)
- Masking tape
- Craft knife
- Metal ruler
- Stripping knife
- Wire brush
- Medium grade sandpaper
- Decorators' brush: 25mm (1in)
- Upholstery staples

The Restoration

Examining the room

If you are restoring a piece of furniture that is destined for a particular room, it is essential that you find out what the style, colour schemes, and textures in that room are. Armed with this information, you can then co-ordinate your project with the room's décor.

For example, the room that this chair is intended for is a modern, large, bright, airy hallway. The carpet is a rose pink. The woodwork of the skirting board has been painted white and the doors are varnished with African mahogany. The wallpaper also has a light pink tone.

From this information it will be immediately apparent that certain colour schemes would not be suitable. For instance, unless I wanted to create a 'conversation piece' or alienate my mother-in-law, lemon yellow fabric and ebonized woodwork would not be a good choice.

Buying the fabric

There is one important principle concerning upholstery that I am now going to pass on to you; decide upon and buy the fabric before doing anything else to the furniture. It is a lot easier to match finishes to fabrics than it is to match fabrics to finishes. The order of events that you should follow goes like this:

1. Find the fabric that matches the décor.
2. Match the finish of the woodwork to the fabric décor.

This is priceless information, gained from bitter experience.

I am hoping to give the chair a more contemporary, lighter look in style and tone. Therefore, I need a light-coloured, modern fabric that will fit in with the hall's décor.

To cover the seat and leave a decent 75mm (3in) margin, I needed a 508mm (20in) square. So, a remnant should do. Luckily, my local fabric store were having a half price sale of remnants. Even better luck, the very first piece of material that I picked up suited my needs perfectly. It was an ivory colour, very thick, with a sculpted texture – very sumptuous and very expensive-looking. My mother-in-law was bound to be impressed. I could almost smell the turkey . . .

Unfortunately, that's where my luck ran out. Not only did it look expensive, it *was* expensive. Plus, it was very large, and they were not willing to cut a smaller piece off. For a poor, impoverished furniture restorer, this was too much. It led me to spend the next 30 minutes trawling through the remnants, considering each piece in turn. I eventually found the perfect piece; and costing under £3.

Stripping

I used chemical stripper, a stripping knife and, most importantly, a wire brush to remove all of the finish from the pores of the wood. The stripping operation took 60 minutes. (See Chapter 5, page 28, for information on using chemical stripper.)

It wasn't until I had completed the stripping that I noticed a disparity in the colour of the chair; the top half of the chair is lighter than the lower sections. This is a common occurrence in old furniture: the chair has been sitting in a room that has waist-high windows so that the top has been bleached by the sun, but the lower sections, which have not been exposed, has remained darker.

An experiment with a little sanding showed that the wood becomes lighter after just a few rubs with medium grade sandpaper, so I am going to sand the lower portions of

Fig 12.3 *Brushing on the chemical stripper.*

Fig 12.4 *Sanding off the darker, top layers of wood to match the sun-bleached top of the chair.*

the chair by hand, to give the whole item a homogenous blonde colour.

Now, sanding wood by hand is about as much fun as roller skating on cobbles. I try to avoid it as much as possible, and truth be known, it is rare that it needs to be done.

The process is quite simple. Using medium grade sandpaper, lightly sand over the entire chair, completing one section at a time. Pay particular attention to the sides of the seat area: during stripping, these will probably have developed some rough, splintery edges.

Remember to always sand in the direction of the grain.

The sanding experiment that I conducted earlier suggested that the job would be quite easy. I estimated that it should take no more than 30 minutes to complete. However, as with most of my best laid plans, this was not to be. Some parts of the chair, notably the areas that are closer to the ground, proved to be more deeply stained than the part upon which I had experimented. In addition, the turned legs were exceptionally fiddly. Consequently, an hour and a half later, I was just finishing the job. If there is a spirit of furniture restoration out there, I had obviously upset it at some time in the past.

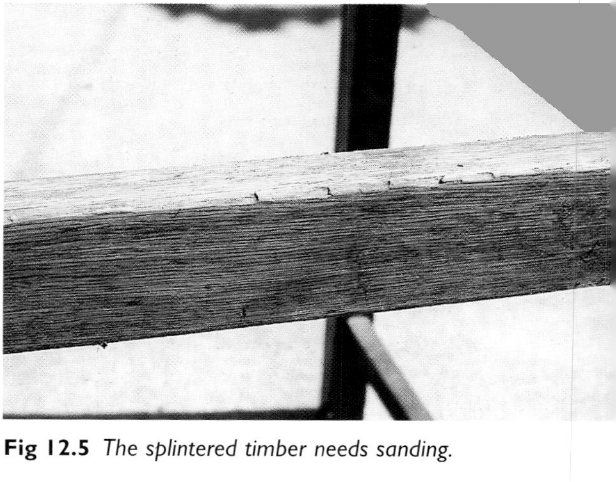

Fig 12.5 *The splintered timber needs sanding.*

Re-covering the seat

The drop-in seat is a common form of upholstery for dining room chairs. Replacing the fabric that covers them is a simple process that can rejuvenate and change a set of chairs beyond all recognition.

The upholstery on this chair is of the most basic and cheapest type. Surprisingly, although primitive, this method of upholstery is quite comfortable, and as the survival of this example shows, robust. I therefore intend to stick with the original method and just replace the covering fabric.

There are two distinct stages to the re-upholstery process; the dirty and potentially dusty job of stripping the old material, and the clean job of replacing the fabric. It is important to recognize, and to physically separate, the two processes.

Removing the old upholstery

The first stage is to strip off the old, decrepit material. For this seat it was simply a case of carefully tearing off the old fabric by hand. Because the fabric had deteriorated, it came off very easily, revealing signs that the seat had originally been covered in a yellow fabric (as can be seen in Fig 12.6).

The previous upholsterer had not bothered to remove the old tacks from the frame. Apart from one or two ill-placed ones, I am going to follow suit, thereby leaving two sets of redundant tacks in the seat.

I could have spent an interesting half an hour removing the unemployed tacks but frankly, it would not have made for a better job. Unless you have half an hour on your hands or the tacks are causing a big problem, such as weakening the structure of the wood or getting in the way of the new tacks, there is no need to remove them.

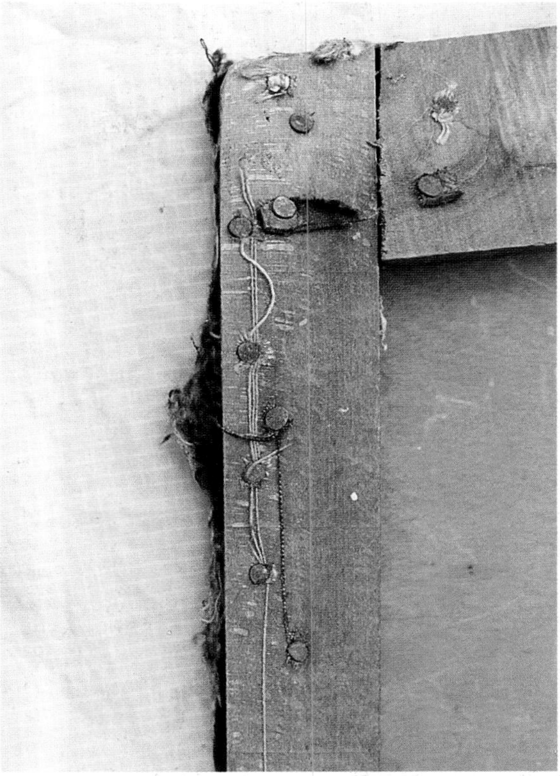

Fig 12.6 *Evidence of a previous, yellow seat covering.*

Replacing the fabric

The second phase of upholstery must be done in a spotlessly clean environment, so find somewhere away from the area in which you do your mucky restoration work. If this is impossible, give your workplace a thorough tidy, sweep down your working area, then wash your hands. With that done, cover your workbench with a clean, old blanket.

Re-covering a drop-in seat is quite simple. If you can wrap a birthday present, this should be a doddle. Place the fabric face down on the covered bench, then lay the seat, with the original wadding in place, on top of this. Ensure that the wadding is all in place and that any pattern on the material is correctly positioned. Fold the fabric over the edges of the seat as though you are wrapping a present, and hold the folds in place using masking tape (see Fig 12.7).

The wrapping must be done tidily, so that when the seat is turned over the whole package looks neat and tidy. Check to see whether the fabric is in the right position, whether the pattern is the right way round, or whether there are any creases. You may need to do this a couple of times to get it just right.

Using masking tape is not the way the professionals do this job, as they have the skill and experience not to bother with this step. But, if like me you only do this every now and again, you will be more interested in getting it exactly right rather than doing it quickly. Using masking tape allows me to adjust the position of the fabric as many times as I wish and check to see that everything is perfectly placed, before finally committing myself to tacks or staples.

Once I had achieved a decent result with the masking tape, I placed the seat in the chair frame to evaluate its effect. The seat simply drops into place and sits on the rebate. This is the time for any second thoughts about the suitability of the material.

Fig 12.7 *'Wrapping' the new fabric covering tidily over the drop-in seat.*

Once you have decided to make a fabric covering permanent, you can secure it with upholstery tacks or staples. Normally I would use tacks to hold the material in position, but a friend lent me a staple gun while I was working on this, so I decided to try that method.

I stapled along one side of the seat without removing the masking tape – this can be removed after the staples or tacks are in. Then, pulling gently and evenly on the opposite side to create tension, I stapled it in place. I repeated this process with the remaining two sides.

Once all four sides were held in position, I folded, tucked and stapled the corners. At this stage the fabric had not yet been cut. With all in position, I removed the tape and trimmed the loose, untidy fabric with a craft knife and a ruler. Don't use a plastic ruler as I did – a metal rule is better. The whole job took about 30 minutes, as everything went well.

Regluing the joint

One of the joints at the top of the chair back was loose. I pulled this joint apart and cleaned off the old glue, in order to reglue it with PVA. I then clamped the joint to hold it in place while it dried. (See Chapter 7, page 50, for more on regluing joints.)

Finishing

Having spent so much time and energy lightening the wood, I did not want to ruin it by giving the chair a finish that darkened the wood more than necessary. Also, I did not want to obscure the texture of the wood. This would be likely if I were to choose a finish that leaves a thick, shiny surface skin on top of the wood.

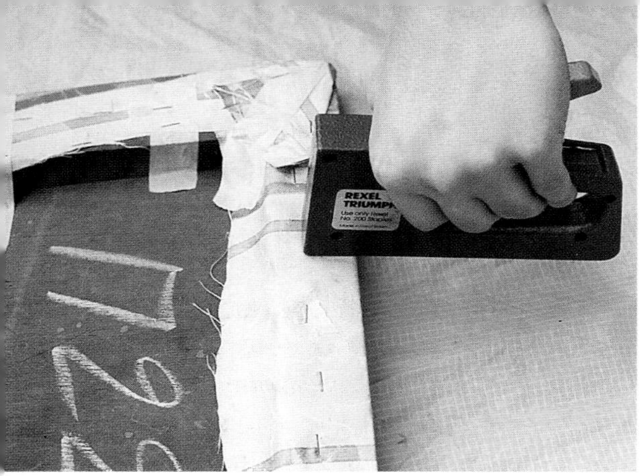

Fig 12.8 *Stapling the fabric into place.*

The finish does not need to be hard-wearing, water- or damp-proof. Given these circumstances I chose the finish more for its aesthetic than its protective qualities, and opted to finish the chair with a water-based, satin acrylic lacquer.

This finish has almost no history, being an invention of the last 20 years, but it has gained many devotees because it is very

Fig 12.9 *Trimming the rough edges on the underside of the seat.*

Fig 12.10 *The re-glued joint was clamped in place while it dried.*

environmentally friendly. It is also very quick and clean to use and relatively cheap, particularly when you calculate the cost of the thinners that are needed to wash brushes used with other finishes.

Water-based lacquers should be applied with a clean, 25mm (1in) decorators' brush, quickly and crisply. Brush the finish out as thinly as possible, working methodically around the chair, and finishing each section completely before moving on to the next. Make sure that you give the underneath of all the sections a coating. Each coat of polish should take no longer than five minutes to apply and, in warm conditions, should be dry within 30 minutes.

Sometimes, where the surface of the furniture is not flat, the finish can take on a soapy quality, leaving a froth on the surface of the wood. If this froth is allowed to dry, the surface will retain a rough texture.

Fig 12.11 *Applying the water-based lacquer.*

To avoid this situation, be sure to dip only the tip of the brush into the finish, and always brush out the finish with the tips of a second, dry brush, so removing any froth.

I gave the chair a second coat after leaving the first to dry for one hour. I did not rub down between coats as a water-based finish, although touch-dry after about 30 minutes, does not achieve full hardness for a couple of days. Rubbing down before it has hardened fully exposes a rubbery texture to the finish that does not sand very well.

However, this is not normally a problem because two coats usually supplies a very quick and pleasant finish which does not need rubbing down if you deal with any 'froth' problems efficiently.

Water-based finishes should not be applied in the damp or cold. In such conditions, they will be slow drying and liable to absorb moisture from the atmosphere, causing the finish to be cloudy. Always apply this type of finish in warm, dry conditions.

Second Thoughts

So there we have it. The wood is finished and it is now a presentable chair, fit for use in a modern home. However, after a moment's reflection on my handiwork I am having doubts. I am not so sure. There is something that I am not happy about.

After further thought and another cup of tea, I identified the problem; it is the amount of pink in the fabric. There is too much. I am now suffering for being a cheapskate and not buying the expensive fabric which I had wanted in the first place. Apart from this, the wood is not the colour I really wanted or expected. Even after all my hard work it went too dark after the finish was applied. I wanted it a lighter shade.

Now, I admit that I am being pernickety, but one of the nice things about doing this sort of work is that you get to please yourself. In fact, that is the main reason for doing it – you are the boss!

I considered stencilling something on those very plain slats at the back, but I think that might go against the austerity of the furniture. It needs just the slightest touch of plain colour to bring the whole thing round.

After much thought, I decided to use ivory paint to highlight some of the woodwork, the idea being to increase the spread of the colour. This should give more prominence to the ivory in the fabric, and because the ivory is spread over a wider area than the pink, it should make the ivory appear more important. That's the theory anyway. Whether it works or not can only be judged after it has been done.

Sometimes trying to decide what to do in these situations can be nerve-wracking. The chair looks alright, it is presentable, but it's not perfect. If I start fiddling with it now, and it goes wrong, the chair and all my hard work could be ruined.

In these situations there is only one question that needs answering: 'What is the worst that can happen?' In this case, if all goes wrong, it is just a simple job of scraping the paint off with a sharp knife and touching up with some more acrylic lacquer. Not much risk involved there. Therefore, I am going to go ahead with my plan.

If there is a risk of it ruining previous work, or if what you intend to do is irreversible, then always do a little experiment first to gain extra information, and make a more informed and confident decision. I decided to highlight the sides of the back splat and three of the rings on the front legs.

I mixed a small quantity of white gloss paint with just a dab of yellow to make an ivory colour, and applied two coats of this

Fig 12.12 *The restored chair, complete.*

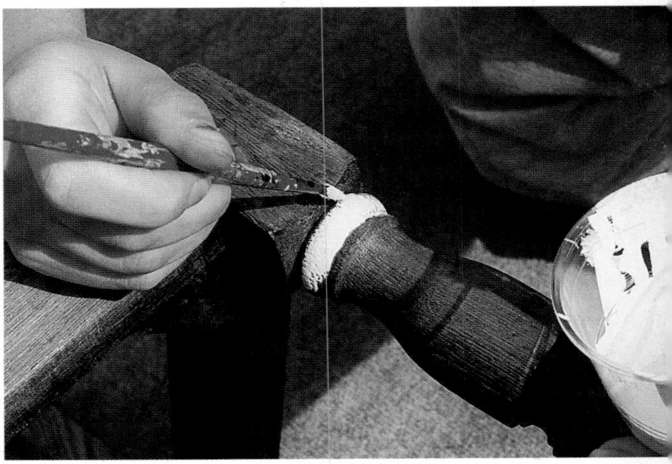

Fig 12.13 *Applying ivory paint to the front leg.*

with an artists' brush. Because the paint was applied over acrylic lacquer, it had poor adhesion, so I gave the painted areas another couple of coats of white polish to seal it in.

You do need a steady hand for this job. If you had too many gin and tonics the night before, or have been subjected to too many fumes from the french polish bottle, you can always tidy up any rough edges with a sharp knife when dry.

Well it certainly changed the look of the piece. Not only is the ivory colour more prominent, it has given the chair a much more contemporary look.

Unfortunately, at this late stage my wife decided to make an appearance, and cast criticism on the chosen fabric. 'It will never do in my mother's hallway.' I have learnt from past experience not to argue in these matters. However, I got some satisfaction from sending her on the second trip to buy suitable fabric, leaving me in peace.

On this occasion, I suffered from letting my wife interfere. With the new fabric in place the ivory paint didn't look right, so I scraped it off and touched up the affected areas with acrylic lacquer.

All that remains now is to inform the proud mother-in-law and arrange delivery. I had not bothered to tell her that I was working on her chair, as there was every likelihood of flying visits, and worse, multiple phone calls dragging me out of the workshop only to inform me that I should be in the workshop getting on with her chair.

In retrospect, perhaps I should have informed her: when I eventually made the call, I was immediately greeted with the disheartening exclamation that they had decided to move house.

On further questioning she told me that the new hallway was small, dark and with not

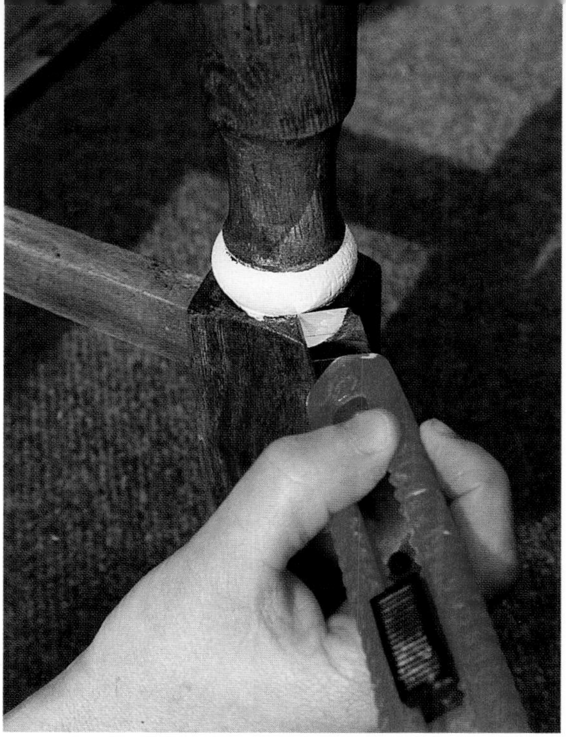

Fig 12.14 *Tidying up the rough edges.*

Fig 12.15 *The painting completed.*

the least bit of pink, but rather more traditional, antique-looking. And then she asked, 'When you finally get around to working on that telephone chair you are always promising me ... would it be possible to make it fit in with this antiquey style?'

After a moment's pause to bang my head against the floor, and while trying not to let my contorted face affect my voice, I said placidly, 'What ... perhaps ... like something, dark brown with red leather upholstery?'

'Oooooooh, yes. That would be perfect,' she cooed.

The finished chair, having gone through many changes from its original form, inset.

CHAPTER 13

Wardrobe

FINISH: PAINT

Often furniture becomes so damaged, with the wood in such a poor state, that it is not feasible to return it to a presentable condition and the only option is to cover the wood up. One way to do this is through ebonizing, as we saw in Chapter 10. Another way is to paint. Sometimes all that is needed is a couple of coats to make the furniture sing. Sometimes two or three different colours are needed to make the furniture come alive.

Fig 13.1 *The badly damaged wardrobe.*

Probably the most versatile decorating medium known to the woodworker is paint, yet in some quarters it is scorned as the ruination of a piece of wood. There is a certain amount of truth to this. Wood has its own beauty that, ideally, we should try to preserve and not obscure. However, paint has so many positive qualities that only a woodaholic would reject it outright.

Paint has a well-earned place in the restorers' artillery. Indeed, some areas of the house cry out for the painted surface – the conservatory, the kitchen, bathroom and nursery – not only for the decorative effects that can be achieved but also for the protection that it can offer furniture from damp, scratches, heat and other abuses.

My first advice to anyone considering using paint is, try and keep it as simple as possible. My second is, always respond to the furniture and the environment that it is to be placed in.

My third is, don't worry. The best thing about paint is that it is foolproof. You cannot go wrong. If you make a complete mess of it, paint over the top.

If you are still worried that you might ruin a piece of furniture with your paint, choose a project that is destined for the scrap heap.

CONCERNING *Wardrobes*

Wardrobes are the ugly sisters of furniture restoration. Nobody wants them, though in many older houses they were and are essential items. Usually, they are large, cumbersome, ugly things, often finished with traditional dark brown polish.

Junk dealers have very little time for wardrobes. If they are of good quality then they have the specific gravity of a battleship, require a rugby team to move them, and take up enormous quantities of space in the shop. If they are of poor quality, they will break up as soon as you move them.

In short, it makes far more sense to stock your shop with small cabinet furniture. It's much more profitable, quicker selling and easier to move and store.

Having said all that, the wardrobe is an essential household item, and they are always to be found if you look hard enough for them.

CONCERNING *This Wardrobe*

The first thing to notice about this piece of furniture is that it has fallen to bits. When I was first offered the wardrobe it was in one piece and standing in the hall of my daughter's nursery. I took it immediately, with no consideration as to where I would keep it until it could be restored. Consequently, it spent a couple of months, neglected, under a tarpaulin in my front garden, with the damp eating away at the glue, lifting the veneer and springing the joints.

The second thing to notice is its unabashed cheapness. It is light and cheaply manufactured, using scanty and poor materials. In most cases, such qualities would definitely consign a piece to the skip. However, this wardrobe has one important and invaluable quality; it is just the right size for Alice's bedroom. Ever since Joanna received the mahogany Chest of Drawers in Chapter 8, Alice, my younger daughter, has been nagging me for her own exclusive and individual wardrobe. Anything that is free, stops my daughter from nagging, and gives me peace takes on incalculable value.

This wardrobe is unusually narrow. The backs, sides and door are made from 3mm (⅛in) oak-faced plywood and the carcase is composed of fruitwood. It was manufactured in 1960 by a firm called Chancellors. I am not flaunting my knowledge of cheap, post-war furniture here; this information is freely available on the plastic tag pinned to the carcase above the door. If only all furniture were so easy to identify!

The original factory-applied finish is an early type of cellulose finish. At some time this has been overlaid with a coat of gloss white paint. This has then had a number of children's illustrations (cut from books or greetings cards) stuck on, as is the fashion with nursery furniture. The door has a rather garish brass-plated knob, and a hasp has been applied for security.

Fig 13.2 *Identification made easy.*

Fig 13.3 *The wardrobe's 'decorative' features.*

The Brief

I want to return this cupboard to a usable state. The idea is to finish up with a cupboard painted to reflect my daughter's tastes and the décor of her bedroom. At the moment this has yellow walls, blue paintwork and white trim, with the usual assortment of unsubtle bright and primary colours that are traditional in a young person's bedroom.

The Plan of Action

1. Reassemble with modern glues.
2. Strip off old finish.
3. Paint.
4. Replace door furniture.

TOOLS AND MATERIALS

For This Wardrobe

(approx.)

- Car body filler, 100ml (3½ fl oz)
- Water-based, non-toxic paint, 400ml (14 fl oz)
- PVA glue, 50ml (1¾ fl oz)
- Black marker pen
- Medium grade sandpaper
- Chisel: 25mm (1in)
- Nails
- Orbital sander

The Restoration

Reassembling

We learnt in Chapter 8, with the mahogany Chest of Drawers, that it is often best to glue furniture together before stripping. The idea is that the old finish will provide a measure of protection for the wood against glue drips and possible damage from clamps.

Following this, my first job was to glue and reassemble the door. This had deteriorated into three sections of frame and the oak-faced ply that composed the middle panel of the door. The last section of the frame was still screwed to the carcase, so I removed this before starting to scrape the old glue from the rebates with a 6mm (¼in) chisel. I then laid all the sections of the door on the ground before assembling them, without glue.

This procedure is known as a dry run. A dry run is essential. It ensures that you have everything in the right place and the right way round, that you have all the clamps and other tools required, and that everything fits and looks O.K. before you finally commit yourself to gluing and clamping.

Once everything was in place, I applied the PVA glue and assembled the furniture permanently.

Some of the corners had suffered from the rainwater that had found its way under the tarpaulin, ungluing the joints and lifting the veneers (see Fig 13.4). I used a somewhat unrefined approach to fix these areas. I slipped glue in between the veneers and pushed it into the joints. I then clamped the wardrobe to draw all the parts into contact, and simply nailed it together. This approach is only possible because the wardrobe is to be painted, so all the nails will be hidden.

Fig 13.4 *Rainwater has damaged the corners and lifted the veneer.*

Fig 13.5 *Clamping and nailing the veneers into place: an unorthodox but effective repair.*

Stripping

Before I decided to take on this restoration, I made one vital investigation regarding the finish. I inspected the surface to see whether the white paint had been properly applied. When I scraped the paint, it fell away with ease. This indicated that it had been applied over the original finish, which makes the job of stripping many hundred times easier.

Fig 13.6 *Having been applied over a cellulose finish, the paint is now flaking off.*

If the old factory-applied cellulose finish had been removed before the white paint was applied, the project may have been unviable. The paint would have been deeply embedded in the open grain of the oak. This would have stopped any flaking, but would also have made stripping a very difficult operation, involving copious amounts of chemical stripper and lots of vigorous scrubbing with a wire brush.

It is rare that I use scraping as a stripping technique but as I have been saying, every piece of furniture is different. You cannot approach restoration with fixed processes or thinking. Respond to the furniture and your brief and be flexible.

With a 25mm (1in) chisel, I scraped the side of the wardrobe and great swathes of white paint and the deteriorated underlying finish were released from the surface. With each scrape another sweep of paint was removed. I keep a number of old chisels just for this type of operation. The trick is to keep them as sharp as possible. Because the

Fig 13.7 *Simply scraping cleared away great swathes of the paint and underlying finish.*

wardrobe has lots of flat sides and no complicated carved or fiddly bits, I had it completely stripped in under two hours.

During the stripping operation, much of the loose veneer at the sides of the wardrobe was removed. I considered sticking the veneers back down as I did for the Bedside Cabinet in Chapter 6, but as the wardrobe was to be painted and the veneers would therefore be unseen, I simply scraped off any damaged or lifted veneer. At the same time, I removed the door furniture. All the screw holes and key holes left from this, and all the areas from which the veneer had been removed, I filled with car body filler.

Once the filler had dried, I smoothed it and the woodwork to perfection with an orbital sander, sanding by hand in the areas that were difficult to reach.

Fig 13.8 *Holes requiring filling were left after all the door furniture was removed.*

Fig 13.9 *Rather than replace missing veneer, I filled the gaps with car body filler.*

Painting

At this stage I was feeling very pleased with myself and more importantly, Alice was feeling very pleased with me. However, Dad has still got to think of a design for the painting operation. As I stripped the furniture, I tried to conjure up an idea that would inspire me to new heights. I considered painting jungle scenes, circus scenes, underwater scenes and balloons, but none of these seemed to excite. As I have stated before, the key to inspiration is to respond to the furniture and the brief.

One thing that hit me immediately about this piece was its long, tall, 'ascending' quality. That and the fin-shaped front legs (see Fig 13.10) conjure up the vision of a rocket.

Now, I said earlier that designers, indeed all of us, are influenced by what is going on in the world around us. This wardrobe was made in 1960, which was around the beginning of the space race. I wonder if this particular designer was influenced, either consciously or subconsciously, by these events? We will never know of course, but a rocket and space scene painted on the wardrobe certainly fits and, more importantly, inspires me to start work with enthusiasm.

Unless you are an experienced artist, confident in your creativity, the one rule I have for you is this; keep it simple. Large blocks of simple, flat colour are all you need to do the job. And remember, if you make a complete mess of it you can always paint over your mistakes.

My first step was to lightly sketch the outline of the rocket shape onto the wardrobe. I used a colander as a template for the three yellow window shapes.

My second step was to 'block in' the basic colour schemes and shapes of the design. All of the paints I used were classified by the manufacturers as being non-toxic and safe for use on toys and children's equipment. They were mostly water-based paints. I used black marker pen for the outlines and filled in the shapes with one coat of the desired colour so that I could get a rough, overall picture of the image. At this stage there was no point in getting too fussy over straight edges or neatness. I was just interested in seeing if the balance of colours and shapes looked okay. If they didn't, it would have been quite simple to change the colour by overpainting. However, the colour scheme being childlike and unsophisticated, it worked very well first time and didn't need adjustment.

Once the rough application of paint had passed muster I started work on the second,

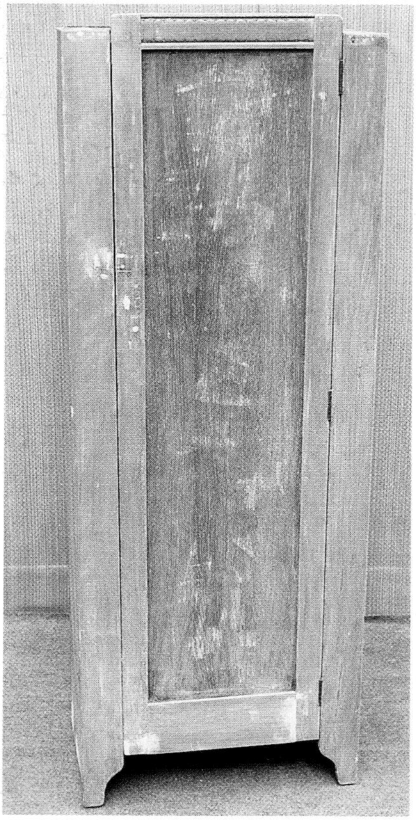

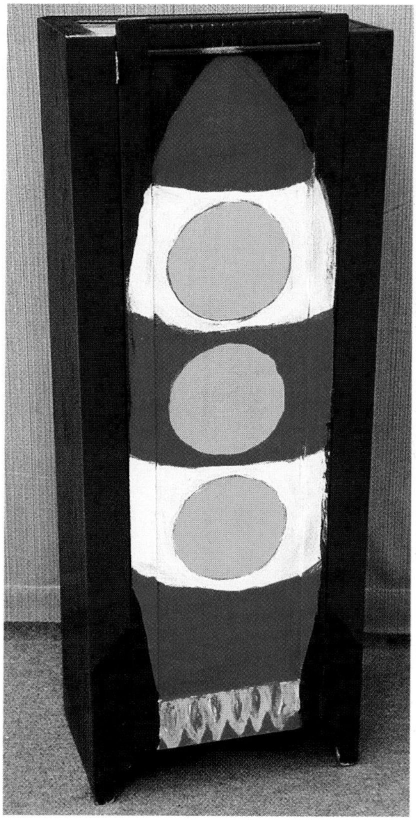

Fig 13.10 *FAR LEFT The tall, narrow shape of the wardrobe inspired the rocket design.*

Fig 13.11 *LEFT The basic colour scheme is roughly blocked in.*

more exacting coat, straightening lines and ensuring that everything had an even coating of colour. I finished off by painting silver stars and a red crescent moon on the sides of the wardrobe. It isn't essential to paint the inside of furniture, but on this occasion I thought it worth the trouble, so I painted the inside blue to match the outside.

When advising the best technique for applying paint, I always suggest that you think of paint as varnish with colour added, and apply the same procedures and techniques. However, something like this does not require a perfectly gloss finish. Indeed, I think it could look wrong if the finish was too preciously applied.

By emphasizing the brushstrokes, I gave the surface of this finish a certain coarse texture. This reflects the fact that it is not intended to be a fine piece of furniture – more a fun piece.

Replacing the door furniture

To finish the wardrobe all that was needed was to screw the new door knob and two small ball catches to the door.

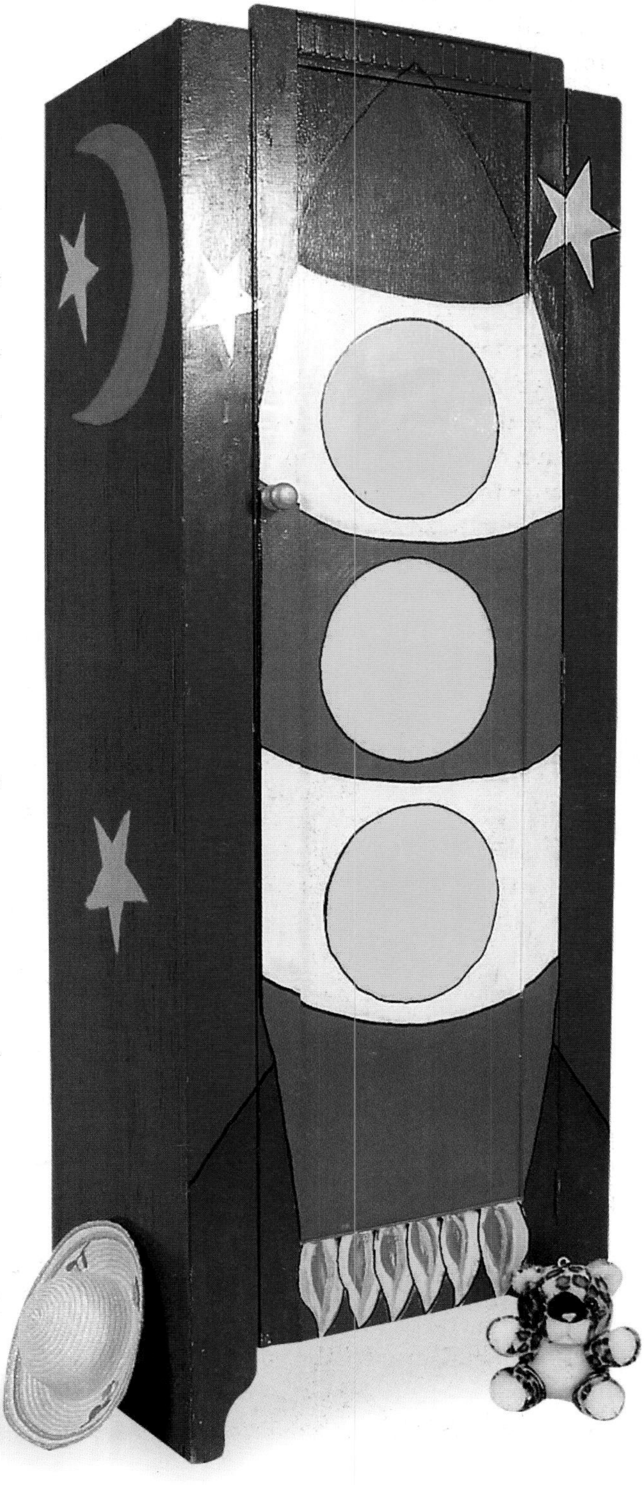

The appalling condition of the wood, inset, is hidden by the finished, painted design.

CHAPTER 14

Sideboard/ Bookcase

FINISH: LIMING WAX

I have stated at other points in this book that we should steer clear of furniture with parts that need replacing, as this work usually requires the skills of a cabinetmaker and can be very expensive.

So what better way to end this book than with a contradiction. This contradiction illustrates a fundamental principle about furniture restoration and indeed, any other creative endeavour – rules are made to be broken (if you have good enough reasons).

The bookcase is perhaps the most sought after item in the junkshop. Historically, books were expensive and in short supply, and a collection of books needing a specific piece of furniture for storage was a rarity found only in the most well-to-do home. In the twentieth century the explosion of the printed word created a demand for books and bookcases. Unfortunately, although bookcases are relatively simple pieces of furniture, they are also rare. Even the most tatty examples can be very expensive. However, if you can't find what you are looking for at the junk shop, how about adapting an existing piece of furniture to your needs?

This sideboard was retrieved from a friend's house. He had just moved in and this had been left in a corner of the garage. My friend offered it to me thinking that I might wish to restore it. I couldn't see much merit in the project; the veneered top was lifting, the doors had been broken off, and it had been half-heartedly vandalized with white paint. However, I accepted the gift. I intended to use it as a temporary work bench while restoring other pieces of furniture in the garden. I planned to restore smaller pieces of furniture on the top and store all my necessary finishes and tools in the cabinet area below. As soon as it had served its purpose or had been picked to pieces by the weather and my ill-treatment, I planned to burn it.

So it was used and abused all summer long. It stayed out of doors, storing my equipment, being punished by the elements

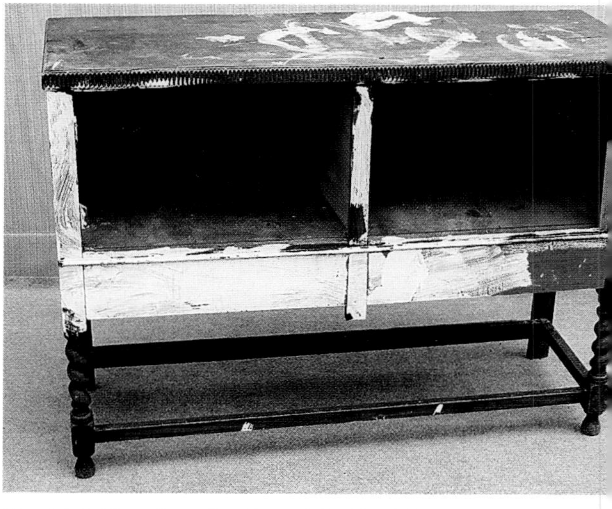

Fig 14.1 *The abused and vandalized sideboard.*

Fig 14.2 *The poor condition of one of the sides.*

and helping me to restore most of the projects in this book.

It's funny how these things happen. I have said before that it is not until you spend some time with furniture that you start to see what's really there. In the beginning I was quite certain there was no point in restoring this piece. My mind was made up. However, over a number of weeks I slowly started to appreciate the qualities of this sideboard and to recognize its possibilities. The rest, as they say, is history.

CONCERNING *Sideboards*

There are many sideboards in the world. Once upon a time they were a standard item, to be found in every household. Sideboards were originally a dining room item, used for storing cutlery, plates, napkins, condiments and all the paraphernalia of the eating ceremony. Originally this stuff was kept on a board of wood by the side of the table, from whence the name derived. Over the centuries, the design has been developed and evolved. Most of the examples that I see on my travels are enormously heavy and ponderously designed, often with turgid carving and bulbous excrescences. I can think of many examples in relatives' homes that have been sitting in the same spot for decades due solely to their weight. They are, without doubt, disgusting examples of the furniture designer's art. For this reason they suffer the same fate as the wardrobe in that there is little second-hand market for them.

CONCERNING *This Sideboard*

Having characterized sideboards in this way, I am now going to work on a completely different example; almost the antithesis of those old battleships. It is small and light with very little decoration except some interesting moulding that imparts an Elizabethan look to it. But its most important feature is that I can imagine the sideboard being easily transformed into an attractive and useful extra bookcase.

Once the remains of the doors are removed, the two inside cabinet areas and the top surface will make excellent spaces for book storage.

The top and sides are made from thin plywood with an oak veneer. The veneers on the top are in a poor condition. In many places around the edge of the top, and in some areas in the centre of the panel, the veneer has lifted. In some places the veneer is missing, and these areas will have to be filled.

The carcase is solid oak. The legs at the front have been turned with a barley twist decoration. These add an element of interest to the design, but also give me pangs of doubt as I am still recovering from the eight barley twist legs of the Drop-Leaf Table in Chapter 7.

Fig 14.3 *The remains of the doors.*

TOOLS AND MATERIALS

For This Sideboard/Bookcase

(approx.)

- Chemical stripper, 250ml (9 fl oz)
- Methylated spirit, 250ml (9 fl oz)
- White spirit, 50ml (1¾ fl oz)
- Car body filler, 50ml (1¾ fl oz)
- White gloss paint, 20ml (¾ fl oz)
- Spirit stain, 1tsp
- Oil stain, 1tsp
- French polish, 250ml (9 fl oz)
- Clear wax, 200ml (7 fl oz)
- PVA glue, 2tsp
- Cloths
- Towelling
- Craft knife
- Wire brush
- Brush: 50mm (2in)
- Screws
- Drawer handle knobs
- Picture frame moulding
- Far Eastern ply/Oak-veneered ply
- Domestic iron

The Brief

My final brief is to turn this decrepit and irretrievable sideboard into a simple receptacle for books. I have already decided to give this project a limed oak finish. This is one of my favourite finishes. I rarely get an opportunity to use it as it looks quite exotic and as a consequence some people are, quite rightly, a little scared of its impact in what might otherwise be a conservatively decorated room. However, this piece is being restored to tickle my taste buds and since it is the last project in the book, I am going to let my hair down and indulge myself a little.

The Plan of Action

1. Remove remains of door.
2. Strip off old finish.
3. Scrub wood to emphasize grain texture.
4. Fix veneers and fill holes.
5. Stain with spirit stain.
6. Apply liming wax.

The Restoration

Removing the door remains

At one time, this sideboard had two doors to enclose the cupboard space. These have been brutally broken off at some time in the past, leaving the hinges and part of the doors in place to tell the tale. I removed these straight away because, as well as being visually offensive, they were physically dangerous – I kept catching my elbow on them.

Stripping and scrubbing

The finish is the standard, dark brown french polish finish that we have encountered in many of the projects in this book. This has been overcoated in many places with white gloss paint. The painting does not appear to be a serious attempt to refinish the furniture, but more like someone cleaning a brush or testing a colour.

Either way, it looks a complete mess. I tried to scrape off the white paint in the same manner that I dispatched the painted finish from the wardrobe. This did not work. Perhaps the paint was of a slightly different chemical composition or, more likely, it was freshly applied paint and therefore still relatively soft. I resorted once again to chemical stripper (see Chapter 5, page 28).

I started with the top, then turned the sideboard on its ends to strip the side panels and carcase. I removed the mouldings, which were just nailed into place with small panel pins, so that I could strip more effectively behind them and scrape away the old glue. It's amazing what effect those mouldings have: without them the whole piece looks very boring.

Fig 14.4 *Removing the mouldings to facilitate stripping.*

I then moved on to the odd-looking panels underneath the cabinet areas. It was here that I started to get a true picture of what the original piece of furniture looked like. Once stripped, it was obvious that those two panels were not oak and were certainly not part of the original furniture. They had been tacked on by a misguided amateur. Moreover, they were very poorly cut. The grain of the left-hand panel ran top to bottom whereas, on the right-hand panel, it ran side to side. Although the finish I had in mind will cover many indiscretions, it could not cope with this sort of aberration. I prised the panels off with the intention of replacing them with better-quality board.

Once they were removed, I could see why they were there in the first place. It is marvellous how clearly you can see with hindsight. It seemed natural now that there should be drawers in the sideboard, and that is exactly what was revealed behind the boards – space for two drawers.

I certainly did not want to get involved in making new drawers for my evolving bookcase, so I resolved to make two new, but more carefully cut panels and leave it at that.

Stripping the top and side revealed two circular holes, obviously made by a large drill, poorly filled with car body filler and then painted. From these little clues I am now getting the impression that at some time in the past somebody had made a half-hearted attempt at restoration. I imagine, judging by the evidence, that this person had a psycho-pathic hatred of sideboards, or perhaps they were just very, very, angry.

Once the sideboard had been stripped, I needed to emphasize and amplify the coarse grain of the oak. This I did by giving the wood a thin coating of stripper and then vigorously scrubbing the wood, systematically scrubbing each section of the sideboard with an engineers' wire brush. This opened up and accentuated the grain as well as cleaning out the old finish in preparation for the limed finish. The attacking action also imparts a time-worn look to the wood that adds to the overall effect.

Replacing the panels

After stripping and scrubbing, I was left with an extra item for the plan of action: replace the panels under the cabinet space.

I had wanted to replace the panels with 3mm (1/8in) oak-veneered ply. However, after phoning a number of timber merchants three things became clear. First, I would have to buy a whole 2.5 x 1.5m (8 x 4ft) sheet of ply. Second, no-one had it in stock. Third, it was far too expensive for a cheapskate like me. After all, I think we have established that one of the joys of restoring junk furniture is achieving your aims with little or no financial outlay. I searched through my pile of wood-that-may-one-day-be-useful, but couldn't find any oak that matched.

I had two options in the woodpile; birch-faced ply or Far Eastern ply. By this I mean simply ply that has been sourced from the Far East. It is often cheaper and of poorer quality than European ply, but it can show exotic timbers on its face. Experiments with a wire brush and some liming wax suggested that the Far Eastern ply would be best. I therefore cut two pieces to the required size with an electric jigsaw, planed the edges true with a small plane, then glued and pinned them into position.

Fixing the veneers and holes

Broken and bubbled veneer is a common problem, as we have already experienced in this book. My first job was to reglue the veneer that had lifted. I did this by slipping a thin spread of PVA glue under the veneer and ironing over the area with a hot iron, as I did with the Bedside Cabinet in Chapter 6. As the glue was pressed out from under the veneer, I wiped it off with a damp cloth. The heat from the iron dried the remaining glue. The whole process took about an hour.

Fig 14.5 *Spreading PVA glue under the areas of lifted veneer.*

Fig 14.6 *Ironing over the veneer to press it into place and fix the glue.*

This left the areas of missing veneer and the holes. I mixed up some car body filler and smoothed it into place to replace the veneers. The holes were a little more difficult. I placed some board behind them to stop the filler falling straight through. As always I had to mix four or five batches of filler, rubbing down previous applications and fine-tuning the surfaces so that they were perfectly smooth. I then took a craft knife and etched into the smooth surfaces a copy of the grain configuration of the surrounding wood (as described in Chapter 7, page 50). I then gave these areas a wipe over with oil stain in order to highlight the etched pattern and gauge the effect.

Fig 14.7 *Etching the grain pattern into the filler.*

Fig 14.8 *Wiping over the filler with oil stain will bring out the pattern that has been etched.*

Staining

We have used spirit stain before (see Chapter 9, page 75), and this operation needs little further explanation. I mixed approximately two teaspoonsful of dark brown spirit stain powder with 280ml (10 fl oz) of meths, and added a splash of french polish to thicken it a little. I brushed it on using a 50mm (2in) brush. Some areas were a little too dark, so I wiped them over with a small section of old towelling dipped in meths. Once I had achieved an even and pleasant colour, I sat back for a well-earned cup of tea, and to evaluate my work.

It was at this stage, meditating upon the furniture, that I realized I should have tried harder with the panels under the cabinet areas. They have to be oak veneer. Nothing else will do. Plus, if I add a couple of knobs to the centre of the panels, they will look like the missing drawer fronts instead of unexplained spaces. And, if I were to frame the outside of the false drawer panels with a little leftover picture moulding, the look would be complete.

The problem was, I didn't have any ply faced with oak veneer. I was almost at the stage of checking down the back of the sofa for loose change to finance the purchase of a sheet of oak-faced ply when I had a bright idea. This material is very common in old furniture. A quick ring around friends and relatives revealed an old oak cupboard in a shed with just what I was looking for. Unfortunately, my friend didn't want to let me have the cupboard as she was using it to store all her gardening equipment. I had to spend quite a lot of time talking her into it. She finally agreed to let me have just one door after I promised to mention her generously in the book. Some people will sell their souls for immortality!

I cut out the panels, glued and screwed some wooden knobs in place, glued and

Tips

Beware! If you don't seal the stain effectively, either because you miss a bit or because the sealer is not thick enough, the stain will leach through and discolour the white wax which is applied after the stain, to give a limed oak look.

Fig 14.9 *Applying the spirit stain.*

Fig 14.10 *The single, oak-panelled door that I bartered for.*

Fig 14.11 *Materials used to transform the panels into 'drawer fronts'.*

pinned the picture moulding into position, gave the 'drawer fronts' a coat of stain and hey presto! The world was right once more.

The next stage was to seal in the stain by applying two coats of thin french polish. This gave the sideboard a slightly glossy finish without filling in the grain as a thicker polish would have done.

The inside of the cabinet is lined with birch plywood rather than oak-veneered ply. I decided to leave this area unlimed to contrast with the rest of the furniture. Consequently, I gave these areas another two coats of french polish as a final finish.

So now we have a sideboard transformed into a bookcase. It has false drawer fronts, a dark brown stain and a brushed french polish finish. We could, if we wished, leave it at that. However, I am looking for something a little more exotic ...

Fig 14.12 *The false drawer fronts in place.*

Applying the liming wax

Liming is a decorative effect that can be achieved in a number of different ways. Perhaps the most common and the easiest way is to buy a special liming wax. This is little more than a white wax. When rubbed onto the surface it can lighten the wood, and if you leave it to build up in mouldings and turnings it can look very attractive. If it is rubbed onto specially prepared, open-grained woods, it will build up in the grain and accentuate its texture and figure, giving the wood a very exotic look.

If you want to be really avante-garde, you can stain the wood any colour you wish and use a complementary colour for the wax. It does not take much imagination to realize that you can combine a whole range of lurid wood stains and waxes to create truly eye popping decorative effects. Pale blue stain with an orange wax works beautifully! But before we get carried away, traditionally the finish is applied to oak and the colour of the liming wax is white.

As I have already mentioned, you can buy ready-made liming wax from DIY shops, but because it is so simple to make, it is almost a sin to make the journey.

Fig 14.13 *Brushing on the liming wax, across the grain.*

Fig 14.14 *Detail of finished liming.*

The recipe I used for this piece combines white gloss paint and clear wax in equal quantities. These are mixed to a smooth paste with a 50mm (2in) brush, then brushed onto the wood across the grain. With the wax applied, I rubbed over the surface with a clean cloth, pushing the white wax mix into the grain at the same time as removing any whiteness from the surface of the wood. This creates the zebra-like pattern typical of a limed oak finish. It is important to change the cloth frequently as it will become saturated with the white wax very quickly.

If the wax becomes hard to shift from the surface, splash a little white spirit on the cloth. If you remove any wax from the grain, all you have to do is apply some more.

I left the limed bookcase to dry overnight before polishing it with clear wax. Oh, and one last piece of advice; since this is essentially an adapted french polish finish, it will take a while for it to become really hard. I do not intend placing any books or other objects on it for at least a week. Just enough time for me to redecorate the room in which it is to be situated. How about a jungle mural, tiger skin throws and a tie-dyed carpet?

False panels and a limed finish have transformed the 'vandalized' sideboard into a presentable bookcase.

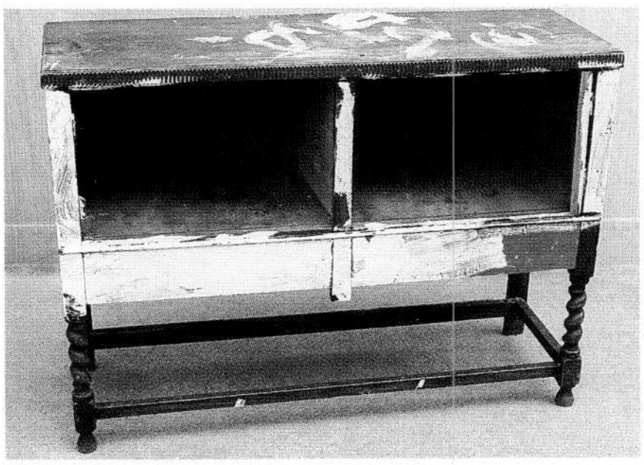

METRIC CONVERSION TABLE

INCHES TO MILLIMETRES AND CENTIMETRES

in	mm	cm	in	cm	in	cm
1/8	3	0.3	9	22.9	30	76.2
1/4	6	0.6	10	25.4	31	78.7
3/8	10	1.0	11	27.9	32	81.3
1/2	13	1.3	12	30.5	33	83.8
5/8	16	1.6	13	33.0	34	86.4
3/4	19	1.9	14	35.6	35	88.9
7/8	22	2.2	15	38.1	36	91.4
1	25	2.5	16	40.6	37	94.0
1 1/4	32	3.2	17	43.2	38	96.5
1 1/2	38	3.8	18	45.7	39	99.1
1 3/4	44	4.4	19	48.3	40	101.6
2	51	5.1	20	50.8	41	104.1
2 1/2	64	6.4	21	53.3	42	106.7
3	76	7.6	22	55.9	43	109.2
3 1/2	89	8.9	23	58.4	44	111.8
4	102	10.2	24	61.0	45	114.3
4 1/2	114	11.4	25	63.5	46	116.8
5	127	12.7	26	66.0	47	119.4
6	152	15.2	27	68.6	48	121.9
7	178	17.8	28	71.1	49	124.5
8	203	20.3	29	73.7	50	127.0

About the Author

Kevin Jan Bonner is an artist, designer, craftsman and teacher. After studying sculpture at art college, he started his own craft/design workshop, specializing in the design and manufacture of award-winning wooden toys. He has also spent many years teaching art and craft subjects at adult education institutes.

This is Kevin's third book, following *Furniture Restoration and Repair for Beginners* and *Furniture Restoration (Practical Crafts)*, also published by Guild of Master Craftsman Publications. He lives in North London.

Index

TITLES AVAILABLE FROM

GMC Publications

BOOKS

Woodcarving

The Art of the Woodcarver	*GMC Publications*
Carving Birds & Beasts	*GMC Publications*
Carving on Turning	*Chris Pye*
Carving Realistic Birds	*David Tippey*
Decorative Woodcarving	*Jeremy Williams*
Essential Tips for Woodcarvers	*GMC Publications*
Essential Woodcarving Techniques	*Dick Onians*
Further Useful Tips for Woodcarvers	*GMC Publications*
Lettercarving in Wood: A Practical Course	*Chris Pye*
Power Tools for Woodcarving	*David Tippey*
Practical Tips for Turners & Carvers	*GMC Publications*
Relief Carving in Wood: A Practical Introduction	*Chris Pye*
Understanding Woodcarving	*GMC Publications*
Understanding Woodcarving in the Round	*GMC Publications*
Useful Techniques for Woodcarvers	*GMC Publications*
Wildfowl Carving – Volume 1	*Jim Pearce*
Wildfowl Carving – Volume 2	*Jim Pearce*
The Woodcarvers	*GMC Publications*
Woodcarving: A Complete Course	*Ron Butterfield*
Woodcarving: A Foundation Course	*Zoë Gertner*
Woodcarving for Beginners	*GMC Publications*
Woodcarving Tools & Equipment Test Reports	*GMC Publications*
Woodcarving Tools, Materials & Equipment	*Chris Pye*

Woodturning

Adventures in Woodturning	*David Springett*
Bert Marsh: Woodturner	*Bert Marsh*
Bill Jones' Notes from the Turning Shop	*Bill Jones*
Bill Jones' Further Notes from the Turning Shop	*Bill Jones*
Bowl Turning Techniques Masterclass	*Tony Boase*
Colouring Techniques for Woodturners	*Jan Sanders*
The Craftsman Woodturner	*Peter Child*
Decorative Techniques for Woodturners	*Hilary Bowen*
Faceplate Turning	*GMC Publications*
Fun at the Lathe	*R.C. Bell*
Further Useful Tips for Woodturners	*GMC Publications*
Illustrated Woodturning Techniques	*John Hunnex*
Intermediate Woodturning Projects	*GMC Publications*
Keith Rowley's Woodturning Projects	*Keith Rowley*
Multi-Centre Woodturning	*Ray Hopper*
Practical Tips for Turners & Carvers	*GMC Publications*
Spindle Turning	*GMC Publications*
Turning Green Wood	*Michael O'Donnell*
Turning Miniatures in Wood	*John Sainsbury*
Turning Pens and Pencils	*Kip Christensen & Rex Burningham*
Turning Wooden Toys	*Terry Lawrence*
Understanding Woodturning	*Ann & Bob Phillips*
Useful Techniques for Woodturners	*GMC Publications*
Useful Woodturning Projects	*GMC Publications*
Woodturning: Bowls, Platters, Hollow Forms, Vases, Vessels, Bottles, Flasks, Tankards, Plates	*GMC Publications*
Woodturning: A Foundation Course (New Edition)	*Keith Rowley*
Woodturning: A Fresh Approach	*Robert Chapman*
Woodturning: A Source Book of Shapes	*John Hunnex*
Woodturning Jewellery	*Hilary Bowen*
Woodturning Masterclass	*Tony Boase*
Woodturning Techniques	*GMC Publications*
Woodturning Tools & Equipment Test Reports	*GMC Publications*
Woodturning Wizardry	*David Springett*

Woodworking

Bird Boxes and Feeders for the Garden	*Dave Mackenzie*
Complete Woodfinishing	*Ian Hosker*
David Charlesworth's Furniture-Making Techniques	*David Charlesworth*
Furniture & Cabinetmaking Projects	*GMC Publications*
Furniture Projects	*Rod Wales*
Furniture Restoration (Practical Crafts)	*Kevin Jan Bonner*
Furniture Restoration and Repair for Beginners	*Kevin Jan Bonner*
Furniture Restoration Workshop	*Kevin Jan Bonner*
Green Woodwork	*Mike Abbott*
Making & Modifying Woodworking Tools	*Jim Kingshott*
Making Chairs and Tables	*GMC Publications*
Making Fine Furniture	*Tom Darby*
Making Little Boxes from Wood	*John Bennett*
Making Shaker Furniture	*Barry Jackson*
Making Woodwork Aids and Devices	*Robert Wearing*
Minidrill: Fifteen Projects	*John Everett*
Pine Furniture Projects for the Home	*Dave Mackenzie*
Router Magic: Jigs, Fixtures and Tricks to Unleash your Router's Full Potential	*Bill Hylton*
Routing for Beginners	*Anthony Bailey*
The Scrollsaw: Twenty Projects	*John Everett*
Sharpening Pocket Reference Book	*Jim Kingshott*
Sharpening: The Complete Guide	*Jim Kingshott*
Space-Saving Furniture Projects	*Dave Mackenzie*
Stickmaking: A Complete Course	*Andrew Jones & Clive George*
Stickmaking Handbook	*Andrew Jones & Clive George*
Test Reports: *The Router* and *Furniture & Cabinetmaking*	*GMC Publications*
Veneering: A Complete Course	*Ian Hosker*
Woodfinishing Handbook (Practical Crafts)	*Ian Hosker*
Woodworking with the Router: Professional Router Techniques any Woodworker can Use	*Bill Hylton & Fred Matlack*
The Workshop	*Jim Kingshott*

Upholstery

Seat Weaving (Practical Crafts)	*Ricky Holdstock*
The Upholsterer's Pocket Reference Book	*David James*
Upholstery: A Complete Course (Revised Edition)	*David James*
Upholstery Restoration	*David James*
Upholstery Techniques & Projects	*David James*

Toymaking

Designing & Making Wooden Toys	*Terry Kelly*
Fun to Make Wooden Toys & Games	*Jeff & Jennie Loader*

Making Wooden Toys & Games — *Jeff & Jennie Loader*
Restoring Rocking Horses — *Clive Green & Anthony Dew*
Scrollsaw Toy Projects — *Ivor Carlyle*
Scrollsaw Toys for All Ages — *Ivor Carlyle*
Wooden Toy Projects — *GMC Publications*

Dolls' Houses and Miniatures

Architecture for Dolls' Houses — *Joyce Percival*
Beginners' Guide to the Dolls' House Hobby — *Jean Nisbett*
The Complete Dolls' House Book — *Jean Nisbett*
The Dolls' House 1/24 Scale: A Complete Introduction — *Jean Nisbett*
Dolls' House Accessories, Fixtures and Fittings — *Andrea Barham*
Dolls' House Bathrooms: Lots of Little Loos — *Patricia King*
Dolls' House Fireplaces and Stoves — *Patricia King*
Easy to Make Dolls' House Accessories — *Andrea Barham*
Heraldic Miniature Knights — *Peter Greenhill*
Make Your Own Dolls' House Furniture — *Maurice Harper*
Making Dolls' House Furniture — *Patricia King*
Making Georgian Dolls' Houses — *Derek Rowbottom*
Making Miniature Gardens — *Freida Gray*
Making Miniature Oriental Rugs & Carpets — *Meik & Ian McNaughton*
Making Period Dolls' House Accessories — *Andrea Barham*
Making Tudor Dolls' Houses — *Derek Rowbottom*
Making Victorian Dolls' House Furniture — *Patricia King*
Miniature Bobbin Lace — *Roz Snowden*
Miniature Embroidery for the Victorian Dolls' House — *Pamela Warner*
Miniature Embroidery for the Georgian Dolls' House — *Pamela Warner*
Miniature Needlepoint Carpets — *Janet Granger*
The Secrets of the Dolls' House Makers — *Jean Nisbett*

Crafts

American Patchwork Designs in Needlepoint — *Melanie Tacon*
A Beginners' Guide to Rubber Stamping — *Brenda Hunt*
Celtic Cross Stitch Designs — *Carol Phillipson*
Celtic Knotwork Designs — *Sheila Sturrock*
Celtic Knotwork Handbook — *Sheila Sturrock*
Collage from Seeds, Leaves and Flowers — *Joan Carver*
Complete Pyrography — *Stephen Poole*
Contemporary Smocking — *Dorothea Hall*
Creating Knitwear Designs — *Pat Ashforth & Steve Plummer*
Creative Doughcraft — *Patricia Hughes*
Creative Embroidery Techniques Using Colour Through Gold — *Daphne J. Ashby & Jackie Woolsey*
The Creative Quilter: Techniques and Projects — *Pauline Brown*
Cross Stitch Kitchen Projects — *Janet Granger*
Cross Stitch on Colour — *Sheena Rogers*
Decorative Beaded Purses — *Enid Taylor*
Designing and Making Cards — *Glennis Gilruth*
Embroidery Tips & Hints — *Harold Hayes*
Glass Painting — *Emma Sedman*
An Introduction to Crewel Embroidery — *Mave Glenny*
Making and Using Working Drawings for Realistic Model Animals — *Basil F. Fordham*
Making Character Bears — *Valerie Tyler*
Making Greetings Cards for Beginners — *Pat Sutherland*
Making Hand-Sewn Boxes: Techniques and Projects — *Jackie Woolsey*
Making Knitwear Fit — *Pat Ashforth & Steve Plummer*
Natural Ideas for Christmas: Fantastic Decorations to Make — *Josie Cameron-Ashcroft & Carol Cox*
Needlepoint: A Foundation Course — *Sandra Hardy*
Pyrography Designs — *Norma Gregory*
Pyrography Handbook (Practical Crafts) — *Stephen Poole*
Ribbons and Roses — *Lee Lockheed*
Rubber Stamping with Other Crafts — *Lynne Garner*
Sponge Painting — *Ann Rooney*
Tassel Making for Beginners — *Enid Taylor*
Tatting Collage — *Lindsay Rogers*
Temari: A Traditional Japanese Embroidery Technique — *Margaret Ludlow*
Theatre Models in Paper and Card — *Robert Burgess*
Wool Embroidery and Design — *Lee Lockheed*

Gardening

Bird Boxes and Feeders for the Garden — *Dave Mackenzie*
The Birdwatcher's Garden — *Hazel & Pamela Johnson*
The Living Tropical Greenhouse: Creating a Haven for Butterflies — *John & Maureen Tampion*

VIDEOS

Drop-in and Pinstuffed Seats — *David James*
Stuffover Upholstery — *David James*
Elliptical Turning — *David Springett*
Woodturning Wizardry — *David Springett*
Turning Between Centres: The Basics — *Dennis White*
Turning Bowls — *Dennis White*
Boxes, Goblets and Screw Threads — *Dennis White*
Novelties and Projects — *Dennis White*
Classic Profiles — *Dennis White*
Twists and Advanced Turning — *Dennis White*
Sharpening the Professional Way — *Jim Kingshott*
Sharpening Turning & Carving Tools — *Jim Kingshott*
Bowl Turning — *John Jordan*
Hollow Turning — *John Jordan*
Woodturning: A Foundation Course — *Keith Rowley*
Carving a Figure: The Female Form — *Ray Gonzalez*
The Router: A Beginner's Guide — *Alan Goodsell*
The Scroll Saw: A Beginner's Guide — *John Burke*

MAGAZINES

WOODTURNING ◆ WOODCARVING ◆ FURNITURE & CABINETMAKING ◆ THE ROUTER
THE DOLLS' HOUSE MAGAZINE ◆ THE SCROLLSAW ◆ BUSINESSMATTERS ◆ WATER GARDENING

The above represents a full list of all titles currently published or scheduled to be published.
All are available direct from the Publishers or through bookshops, newsagents and specialist retailers.
To place an order, or to obtain a complete catalogue, contact:

GMC Publications, Castle Place, 166 High Street, Lewes, East Sussex BN7 1XU, United Kingdom
Tel: 01273 488005 Fax: 01273 478606 *Orders by credit card are accepted*